THE ULTIMATE
COLLEGE
COOKBOOK

Clarkson Potter/Publishers
New York

THE ULTIMATE
COLLEGE
COOKBOOK

Easy,
Flavor-Forward
Recipes for
Your Campus
(or Off-Campus)
Kitchen

VICTORIA GRANOF

Published in the United States by Clarkson Potter/Publishers, an imprint of
Random House, a division of Penguin Random House LLC, New York.

clarksonpotter.com

CLARKSON POTTER is a trademark and POTTER with colophon is a
registered trademark of Penguin Random House LLC.

Library of Congress Cataloging-in-Publication Data

Names: Granof, Victoria, author.

Title: The ultimate college cookbook: easy, flavor-forward recipes for your
    campus (or off-campus) kitchen / Victoria Granof.

Description: New York: Clarkson Potter/Publishers, 2020. | Includes index.

Identifiers: LCCN 2020010644 (print) | LCCN 2020010645 (ebook) | ISBN
    9780593232088 (trade paperback) | ISBN 9780593232095 (ebook)

Subjects: LCSH: Quick and easy cooking. | College students—Nutrition. |
    LCGFT: Cookbooks.

Classification: LCC TX833.5 .G7146 2020 (print) | LCC TX833.5 (ebook) | DDC
    641.5/12—dc23

LC record available at https://lccn.loc.gov/2020010644.

LC ebook record available at https://lccn.loc.gov/2020010645.

ISBN 978-0-593-23208-8

Ebook ISBN 978-0-593-23209-5

Printed in Italy

Book and cover design by Jen Wang

Photographs by Emily Schindler

10 9 8 7 6 5 4 3 2 1

First Edition

To Theo,
    for college and beyond

CONTENTS

INTRODUCTION

If this is your first foray into cooking, fear not, young grasshopper. You made it past the SATs; this is nothing. In cooking, like anything, practice makes perfect—you find what you like and figure out how to do it the way that works for you. Now I know that, being young and brash and clever, you wish to make your own mistakes, but I've made enough of them myself to offer you some good advice. So take it. You can thank me later.

* Cook with your hands. (Wash them first.) In Italian, hands that have cooked and cooked well are called *mani sapienti*—knowledgeable hands. They're your best tool. You'll learn how things should feel and how to stop when you've reached the right texture. You'll learn to measure without tools, and your food will taste like love.

* Cook with good salt and freshly ground pepper. The best ingredients are worthless if you're seasoning them with subpar salt and pepper. Buy whole black peppercorns and put them in a pepper mill (it can be small and the cheapest you can find; it doesn't have to be fancy) to grind them fresh each time you need to.

* Don't skimp on salt. Our bodies are 0.04 percent salt and require it to function. Plus, salt brings out the flavor in food, both sweet and savory. Just remember to drink water.

* Don't skimp on fat. Fat is brain food and fat tastes GOOD.

* Don't be afraid of making mistakes. You gotta just roll with it when that happens, and it *will* happen. Some of the best discoveries started out as mistakes. Besides, that's what garnishes and pretty plates are for.

* Be brave. Go forth and COOK, young grasshopper!

BASIC EQUIPMENT
Outfitting the Little Kitchen That Could

THE LITTLE BIG THINGS

Fads come and go. Beauty fades. *#factsoflife.*

Chances are, if you've entered college any-time after 2018, that along with your twin XL sheets and collapsible laundry bag, someone has given you an Instant Pot that is supposed to Change. Your. Life. Let's be real here. A 4.0 GPA and a paid internship might do that, but not a big clunker of a suburban kitchen appliance (no dis-respect to Instant Pots). It might help if you had a big suburban kitchen and three kids to feed twenty-one times a week, but you're just a smart young thing trying to feed yourself something good on a budget, maybe in a space that's not even meant for cooking.

You def don't need all of these appliances, but even just one of them will up your kitchen cred and preparedness:

ELECTRIC TEAKETTLE: Besides boiling water in three minutes for tea or coffee, an electric kettle will allow you to make soft-, medium-, or hard-boiled eggs, couscous, or steamed veg-etables. (Put your cut-up vegetables in a heat-proof bowl, pour boiling water over them, seal with beeswax wrap or a lid, and leave for a few minutes until cooked to your liking. Drink the water afterward—lots of vitamins in there.) You can also poach fish or chicken (see page 50) and cook rice noodles for salad rolls (page 88) or Bang noodles (page 50).

RICE COOKER: They should rename this, because cooking rice is the least of its charms. It makes perfectly cooked grains (quinoa: 2 parts water to 1 part quinoa; press button; boom), applesauce, mashed potatoes from scratch, chutney (page 148), jam, chocolate ganache (page 142), mac and cheese from the box, one-pot pasta (page 45), potato chip frittata (page 24), lion's head meatballs (page 78), grits, oat-meal, poached fruit, and steamed veg. It also—pro tip—removes the smell of smoke from a room if you simmer two cups of water and a halved lemon in it.

SLOW COOKER: It will do lots of the things a rice cooker will *and* bake a loaf of crusty bread; cook a pot of vegan chili (page 77) or a beef, beer, and bacon stew (page 81); bake a potato (or a sweet potato, page 26); make bone broth, hot spiced cider, hot chocolate, fondue, queso, soup, flan, or dulce de leche (page 133). You can turn it into an aromatherapy humidifier by sim-mering cinnamon, cloves, and orange peel in water, or keep towels warm in it for an at-home spa treatment.

WAFFLE IRON: Even if all this did was make waffles, it would be worth it. With a good store-bought mix, you can make them sweet or savory: add some cheese, dried or fresh fruit, chopped bacon, pepperoni or salami, herbs and spices, chopped up vegetables, chocolate, peanut but-ter, marshmallows—and on and on. BUT you

can also use a waffle iron (even a mini one) to make a banging grilled cheese (page 91), crème brûlée French toast (page 37), brownies, corn bread, refrigerator biscuits, cinnamon rolls, hash browns, scrambled eggs, and quesadillas. And, of course, just plain toast.

ELECTRIC SKILLET: My personal favorite. Think of it as a one-stop-shopping cooktop. You can sauté, fry, deep-fry, make soup, stews, chili, pancakes, pasta, chicken, burgers, steak, fish, scrambled eggs, omelets, ramen, *and* bake in it! Don't believe me? Try the brownies on page 137. And if all that's not enough, use it to heat stones for a hot stone massage—finals week just got a lot easier.

TOASTER OVEN: Not essential, but nice if you plan to do a good bit of baking or broiling. I've tried making my Banana Bread Granola (page 35) and Hot Chocolate Lava Cakes (page 129) in every other appliance, but a toaster oven's best. A small and simple one will do.

MICROWAVE: You don't hugely need one, since any one of the appliances above (except the slow cooker, for obvious reasons) can get you fed in ten minutes or less. How fast do you really need to eat, anyway? The FDA warns that too much exposure to microwaves can cause radia-tion burn, and that's no small deal. If you already own a microwave, I will say that they make great off-season sweater storage and pest-free spice cabinets. And you can make the Paper Bag Popcorn on page 120 if you stand back.

MINI FOOD PROCESSOR/CHOPPER: If you plan to make lots of Vim Balls (page 104) and Crush Bars (page 108), or pesto, chili paste, and Piri Piri Sauce (page 145), this might just be worth it for you. It'll also chop vegetables and make acai bowls, if that's your thing.

BLENDER OR BULLET: I couldn't survive without my blender. From smoothies and sauces to soups, pesto, nut milks, nut butter, and Hack-uccinos (page 116), this is the appliance that keeps me healthy and sane. Buy either the blender or the bullet, but not both. Most blenders will turn any wide-mouthed Mason jar into a bullet. Just unscrew the blender jar and replace it with a Mason jar, blitz, screw on the Mason jar lid, and go!

SURGE PROTECTOR: You never know when you'll want to cook a meal, type a term paper, and blow-dry your hair, all at the same time. *#BePrepared.*

THE BIG LITTLE THINGS

The Best Supplies to Keep Handy to Make Your Life Easier

A set of graduated glass bowls (Pyrex, for example) with lids

Wooden spoon

Silicone spatula

Wire whisk

Short-handled tongs

Measuring cups and spoons

2-cup glass measuring cup

Small cutting board (a wooden one doubles as a cheese board)

Can opener

Pepper mill

Vegetable peeler

A few nice big coffee mugs (bake in them, drink out of them, use them as prep bowls)

Dishes, bowls, and silverware

Cheap paintbrush to use as a pastry brush

Cotton dish towels (can double as napkins when you want to get fancy)

Paring knife

Serrated knife for tomatoes and bread

8-inch chef's knife

Box grater (cheese is cheaper when you grate it yourself)

8 x 6-inch rectangular glass baking dish with lid

A couple of 1/8-size sheet pans

Wide-mouthed Mason jars for drinks, storage, and DIY bullet blender (see page 13)

Nonstick foil

Silicone pan liners

Reusable zipper storage bags

Beeswax food wrap

SIX TECHNIQUES YOU NEED TO KNOW

BOIL: Technically, boiling happens at 212°F. A vigorous boil is good for cooking pasta and green vegetables. What I call a nice happy boil is still hot—195° to 211°F—but the water is moving more slowly. This is good for soups and things like reducing the liquid in the adobo on page 70.

SIMMER: Simmering is when the liquid is just below boiling—180° to 195°F—and the bubbles form and break slowly. This kind of gentle cooking is good for braises, stews, and milk, and helps tenderize meat and develop flavors. I like to call this a lazy boil.

ROAST: Roasting is cooking by indirect heat, uncovered, at a temperature of 400°F or higher to create a browned, flavorful surface on the food being cooked. This technique is good for meat, poultry, some fish, and root vegetables.

BAKE: Baking is also cooking by indirect heat, but at a lower temperature (typically 300°–375°F), and sometimes covered. This is good for more delicate things like cake, cookies, and lasagne.

SAUTÉ: This is what I call cook and stir. To sauté is to cook food quickly in a minimal amount of fat over high-ish heat while keeping it moving. Sauté is the correct term, but I think it sounds a bit pretentious, *n'est-ce pas?* You'll know that the fat is the right temperature when the surface appears to shimmer if you look at it from the side.

SALTING: What I'm about to say is based purely on personal observation, but I believe and stand by it: An American pinch of salt uses two fingers and is approximately ¼ teaspoon. A French pinch of salt uses three fingers and measures approximately ½ teaspoon. And an Italian pinch of salt uses all five fingers and amounts to about a full teaspoon. That is all to say that different people will read "a pinch of salt" differently. You will be instructed to add a pinch of salt in many of the recipes throughout the book. Use your instincts! Again, you shouldn't be afraid to use as much salt as you please, BUT it's wise to start with a small (two-finger) pinch each time, and taste as you go—you can always add more salt later, but it's impossible to rewind the salt if you add too much right away.

A NOTE ON THE RECIPES

You will see symbols next to each recipe for what diets or dietary needs they comply with, including gluten-free, dairy-free, vegetarian, and vegan. If there are options in a recipe's ingredient list, it's the first option that will fit the category listed. (So if a recipe is presented as being gluten-free, tamari will be listed before soy sauce; or if oil is the option before butter, then the recipe could be labeled dairy-free and vegan.) Sometimes a recipe might not be any of these things outright, but there are tips for making simple swaps to convert it to whatever you need it to be. Here is a key for reference:

GF GLUTEN-FREE   **VG** VEGETARIAN   **DF** DAIRY-FREE   **VE** VEGAN

There are also symbols in each recipe that designate which appliances can be used to make it:

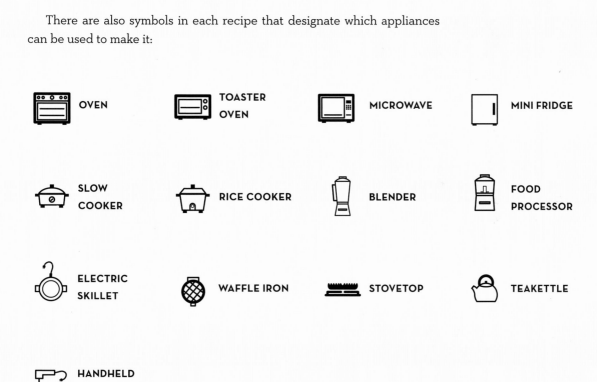

OVEN   TOASTER OVEN   MICROWAVE   MINI FRIDGE

SLOW COOKER   RICE COOKER   BLENDER   FOOD PROCESSOR

ELECTRIC SKILLET   WAFFLE IRON   STOVETOP   TEAKETTLE

HANDHELD MIXER

PANTRY STAPLES

OLIVE OIL: Find a good extra-virgin olive oil you like, and use it everywhere olive oil is called for. No need to buy fancy finishing oils.

VEGETABLE OIL: I like canola or corn oil when a neutral, flavorless oil is called for.

TOASTED SESAME OIL: What I mean here is the dark brown, lusciously fragrant oil pressed from toasted sesame seeds, used in Asian cooking. Available in most supermarkets.

COCONUT OIL: There are all sorts of health benefits to coconut oil that make it worth using when you can. What I like is that it tolerates high temperatures without burning or breaking down. And it tastes good.

SALT AND PEPPER: I use kosher salt in all my cooking; it's pure and clean tasting, and not too salty. As for pepper, invest in a mill and use it; there's no substitute for the brightness and punch of freshly ground peppercorns.

SWEETENERS: I most often use real maple syrup or brown sugar as a sweetener. Agave is a good option, and sometimes honey, in things where its flavor is appreciated.

HEAT: I like spice, but that doesn't always mean burn-your-tongue-off spicy. A little bit of heat keeps your taste buds awake and aware. Cayenne is easy to keep around and it's pretty much all-purpose. I love Chinese chili garlic sauce and the kind of chili oil that has crispy bits of garlic. Also sriracha, harissa, Aleppo pepper, and the kind of red pepper flakes you find at pizza joints are also good to have.

MISO: Miso is one of my favorite ingredients and is one of those ancient healthy fermented foods you should be working into your cooking. Red miso is smoky and full-flavored, while white and light misos are milder and more buttery-tasting. Use whichever you like when a recipe calls for miso.

PASTAS, RICE, AND GRAINS: Buy pasta that's made with semolina or alternative grains, if you prefer. Instant couscous, simple short-grain sushi rice, long-grain rice, and basmati rice are all good to have around. And rice noodles can be cooked just by soaking in hot water. Oats and grits, too. And ramen, *#natch*.

CHICKPEAS: I'm crazy for chickpeas (and even wrote a book about them!). I like to keep chickpea flour (also known as garbanzo bean flour, or besan in Indian markets), canned chickpeas, and dried chickpeas on hand. In dire situations, a fork and a can of chickpeas will bring you back from the edge of *#hangry*.

THINGS IN CANS AND TUBES: Black beans, kidney beans, navy beans, lentils, chickpeas, whole peeled tomatoes, diced tomatoes, tomato paste, coconut milk, red curry paste, sweetened condensed milk, chicken broth, beef broth, and vegetable broth.

VINEGARS: Always keep apple cider vinegar around, definitely. Balsamic vinegar for salads or for a quick finish for meat or tofu. Rice vinegar and distilled white vinegar if you have space. Distilled vinegar is good for cleaning glass and pickling things.

CORNFLAKES: Ever had a cornflake shake? It's just cornflakes, milk, and sweetener, blitzed in a blender. It's one of my guilty pleasures. Cornflakes are in lots of recipes (both savory and sweet!) in this book and are technically a whole grain, so keep a box around.

SPICES AND DRIED HERBS: Ground cumin, coriander, cinnamon, cardamom, garam masala, turmeric, sage, cayenne, curry powder, smoked paprika, garlic powder, oregano, bay leaves, vanilla extract, unsweetened cocoa powder. All of these, particularly the spices, are easy to find online if you can't find them in your local store.

THINGS IN BOTTLES AND JARS: Soy sauce or tamari (which is GF), mirin, instant espresso powder, ketchup, Dijon mustard, mayonnaise, peanut butter, crispy onions (the kind on top of green bean casserole), dashi granules.

DRIED THINGS: Medjool dates, apricots, shiitake mushrooms, raisins, chia seeds, rice paper sheets, seaweed snacks, and matcha or Chinese green tea powder.

BREAKFAST

THE
MOST IMPORTANT
MEAL
OF THE DAY

FOR
BUSY WEEKDAYS
& LEISURELY
WEEKENDS

SHAKSHUKA

Say that three times fast. Shakshuka is a typical Middle Eastern breakfast of eggs baked in a fragrant tomato sauce. Level up with a handful of spinach, chard, or kale stirred in toward the end, and serve with pita chips to sop up all the tomatoey deliciousness.

SERVES 1

1 teaspoon extra-virgin olive oil

Half of a small red or yellow bell pepper, seeded and coarsely chopped

1 garlic clove, halved

½ teaspoon ground cumin

Pinch of red pepper flakes or Aleppo pepper *(optional)*

1 cup Core Tomato Sauce *(page 147)* or your favorite store-bought tomato sauce

1 to 2 large eggs

Yogurt, harissa, and pita chips or crusty bread, for serving *(optional)*

MAKE IT ON THE STOVE: In a small saucepan (with a lid), heat the olive oil over medium-high heat until it shimmers.

Add the bell pepper and garlic and cook, stirring, for a minute or two, until the pepper has begun to soften. Add the cumin, red pepper flakes (if using), and tomato sauce and stir to incorporate. Reduce the heat to medium so that the sauce boils happily but not fiercely, and let it cook, uncovered, for about 5 minutes more, until slightly thickened.

Reduce the heat to low to allow the sauce to simmer, and use a large spoon to push some of the sauce away from the middle and make a small well in the center. Break the egg(s) into a small cup, then tip into the well. (Don't worry if the yolks break; it will all end up in the same place anyway.) Cover the saucepan and let simmer for 3 to 4 minutes more, until the yolks are set but still jammy.

Turn the shakshuka out into a shallow bowl and top with yogurt and harissa, and serve with pita chips or bread for dipping, if you like.

MAKE IT IN A RICE COOKER: Preheat the rice cooker to Cook mode and add the olive oil. Follow the same instructions as above (it will take a few more minutes for the vegetables to cook in the second step).

After you add the egg(s), cover the rice cooker and let the eggs cook until they have reached your desired level of doneness. Continue as above.

POTATO CHIP FRITTATA

This single-serving frittata is perfect as a breakfast for one, and the untraditional addition of potato chips will make you feel like a genius even in the early hours. (Also, making it in a rice cooker is *#lifechanging.*) It's even better at room temperature—slap this on a bun and you have yourself an egg sandwich on the fly. Just don't wrap cooked eggs in foil or they'll turn green—opt for beeswax wrap, a paper bag, or wax paper instead.

MAKES ONE 4-INCH FRITTATA

A small knob of unsalted butter, for the pan

2 large eggs

1 *(1-ounce)* bag of potato chips (I like the sour cream and onion flavor for this)

OPTIONAL ADD-INS

Chopped deli meat, cooked sausage, cheese (*#natch*), leftover cooked veggies, raw spinach, chopped onions, bell peppers, fresh herbs, and chopped tomato—and even smoked salmon if it's in the budget.

MAKE IT ON THE STOVE: Heat a knob of butter in a 4-inch skillet over medium heat. Meanwhile, in a mug or small bowl, whisk the eggs gently with a splash of water until combined. (Don't beat the heck out of them or they'll become rubbery.)

When the skillet is hot and the butter has melted, pour in the egg mixture (and any add-ins, if using) and immediately add the potato chips and use a spatula to press them under the egg mixture until the chips are submerged. It's okay if some float to the top. Let cook, without stirring, about 30 seconds, until you see the edges beginning to set. Use a fork or a small silicone spatula to push the cooked frittata toward the center of the skillet, letting the uncooked portions run to the edges. Keep doing this till there's no more runny egg and the top is still a little jiggly. Remove from the heat to serve, or flip the frittata with a spatula to cook the other side for a few seconds. (It's small—you can do it!)

MAKE IT IN THE RICE COOKER: Preheat the rice cooker on the Cook mode and add a small knob of butter. Meanwhile, in a mug or small bowl, whisk the eggs gently with a splash of water until combined. (Don't beat the heck out of them or they'll become rubbery.)

When the rice cooker is hot and the butter has melted, pour in the egg mixture (and any add-ins, if using) and immediately add the potato chips and use a spatula to press them under the egg mixture until the chips are submerged. It's okay if some float to the top.

Cover the rice cooker and let cook for 8 minutes (meanwhile, go make your bed or do something that'll keep you busy). When the frittata is done, the rice cooker will automatically switch to the Warm mode, and the frittata will be set around the edges with just a bit of runniness in the middle.

#SLOMO SWEET POTATO
WITH MISO BUTTER

Betcha didn't know you could bake a potato in your slow cooker, am I right? Who wouldn't love one of those with good salty butter or some Greek yogurt for breakfast? Sweet potatoes are packed with nutrients to help you stay bright and brainy till lunch, and they become even sweeter when cooked slowly overnight. The Miso Butter strikes just the right sweet-salty-smoky balance. You can easily scale this up to make more than one at a time—just limit it to however many potatoes can fit in the slow cooker in one layer.

SERVES 1

1 medium *(10-ounce)* **sweet potato or yam, washed and patted dry**

Toasted sesame oil

Kosher salt

Miso Butter, for serving *(recipe follows)*

MAKE IT IN A SLOW COOKER: Preheat the slow cooker to High or Low, depending on how long you'd like the potato to cook.

Meanwhile, rub the potato all over with the oil and salt. Wrap it loosely in foil and place it in the slow cooker. Cook on High for 4 hours or Low for 6 to 8 hours. That's IT. Remove from the slow cooker, slice the potato in half lengthwise, and top with the miso butter. (Remember to reuse the foil as many times as you can!)

MAKE IT IN THE OVEN: Preheat the oven to 425°F.

Rub the potato all over with the oil and salt and place it on an ⅛-size sheet pan. Bake until the potato is tender when pierced with a fork, 45 to 55 minutes. Slice the potato in half lengthwise, and top with the miso butter.

NOTE *Miso often contains gluten, so if you need to make this gluten-free, just skip over the miso butter and use the sweet potato as a canvas for a multitude of other toppings.*

VG Miso Butter

MAKES ABOUT 1 CUP

Miso, the Japanese soybean paste that lends a salty-umami flavor to everything it graces with its presence, is blissfully easy to find these days, whether in your everyday supermarket or online. This recipe makes more than you'll need for one sweet potato, but you can use it on roasted carrots, squash, eggplant, and even corn on the cob. Add the cayenne if you like things a little spicy. This will keep, covered, in the fridge for up to 1 month.

¼ cup miso *(any type)*

½ cup *(1 stick)* **unsalted butter, at room temperature**

1 teaspoon **toasted sesame oil**

3 tablespoons **maple syrup, brown sugar, or agave**

Pinch of **cayenne** *(optional)*

In a small bowl, use a spoon or small silicone spatula to combine the miso and the butter until well blended and creamy. Add the sesame oil, maple syrup, and cayenne (if using), and continue to blend until the mixture is smooth and homogeneous.

CH-CH-CH- CHIA PUDDING

I love foods that go *pop* in your mouth, like bubble tea, grapes, and the chia seeds in this pudding. Chia pudding needs no cooking, just a few hours in the fridge to let the chia seeds absorb the liquid and thicken it up. Sub in mashed soft fruit like berries or peaches for the milk, use half the amount of seeds, and you have a super-healthy fruit spread. You will need two clean 8-ounce jars (such as Mason jars) with lids—not only do these jars make it easy to prep the puddings ahead of time, they're also perfect for a grab-and-go breakfast if you're running straight to class in the morning!

SERVES 2

2 cups plant-based milk, such as coconut, almond, or oat

Pinch of kosher salt

1 teaspoon vanilla extract

3 tablespoons agave, honey, or maple syrup *(optional)*

6 tablespoons chia seeds *(white or black)*

In a small bowl, whisk the milk, salt, vanilla, and agave (if using). Add the chia seeds and whisk until no lumps remain.

Pour the mixture into two 8-ounce jars, cover with the lids, and refrigerate until thick, at least 3 hours or overnight. The pudding will keep, tightly covered in the fridge, for up to a week.

Variations

PINA COLADA: Use coconut milk and substitute 3 tablespoons of dark brown sugar for the other sweeteners. Add about ½ cup of chopped or crushed fresh pineapple to the chia mixture.

CHERRY CHAI: Add 2 to 3 tablespoons of instant chai latte powder to the milk mixture before you add the chia. Stir in a handful of dried tart cherries or a few halved fresh cherries, if you have them (no pits!).

CINNAMON BUN: Add 1 to 2 teaspoons of cinnamon and a pinch of grated nutmeg to the milk mixture before you add the chia. Substitute 3 tablespoons of dark brown sugar for the other sweeteners and add an additional ½ teaspoon of vanilla.

ALL-NIGHTER OATS

VG

While you're pulling an all-nighter, so is this oatmeal. It "cooks" in the fridge while you cram for those midterms. Next morning, grab it and go. It's good cold or at room temperature, or warmed up right in the jar. Just like for the Ch-Ch-Ch-Chia Pudding (page 28), it's best to use two clean 8-ounce jars (such as Mason jars) with lids to prepare this make-ahead breakfast.

SERVES 2

½ cup regular (*not quick-cooking*) **rolled oats**

1 cup milk or plant-based milk

1 to 2 tablespoons maple syrup, agave, or honey (*optional*)

Pinch of kosher salt

In a medium bowl, combine the oats, milk, and the maple syrup, as desired. Add a pinch of salt and stir.

Divide the oats mixture between two 8-ounce jars. Cover both jars with their lids and refrigerate overnight. When you're ready to eat, top the oats with fresh fruit, nuts, nut butter, all-fruit preserves, seeds, yogurt, chocolate chips, cocoa nibs—whatever you like.

TIP *Make this vegan by using plant-based milk instead of regular milk, and/or make it gluten-free by using certified gluten-free oats.*

Variations

BANANA BREAD: Mash a ripe banana with a fork. Add the mashed banana and 1 teaspoon of vanilla extract to the oat mixture and stir to incorporate. After refrigerating, top the oats with some chopped walnuts and crushed banana chips, or a sliced banana.

APPLE PIE: Grate or chop 1 apple and add half of it to the oat mixture. Add 1 teaspoon of cinnamon, a pinch of nutmeg, and 1 teaspoon of vanilla extract and stir. After refrigerating, top the oats with the remaining chopped apple.

PUMPKIN SPICE OATS (#PSO): Add a few tablespoons of pumpkin purée (fresh or canned), 1 teaspoon of pumpkin pie spice blend, and 1 teaspoon of vanilla extract to the oat mixture and stir to combine. After refrigerating, top the oats with vanilla yogurt and chopped pecans. [Tip: Use the remaining pumpkin purée in a Power-Up Shake (page 112) or in the Hack-uccino (page 116).]

GRITS, EGGS & GREENS

This recipe is just enough for a 2-cup rice cooker. If you have a larger one, just scale up the amounts proportionately. Always break your eggs into a smaller cup first; the last thing you want to be doing in the morning is fishing bits of eggshell out of your grits. You're welcome.

SERVES 1

¼ cup quick-cooking grits

½ tablespoon unsalted butter

Pinch of kosher salt, plus more to taste

Freshly ground black pepper

Handful of baby spinach

2 tablespoons grated Cheddar cheese

1 to 2 large eggs

Hot sauce, for serving (optional)

MAKE IT ON THE STOVE: In a small saucepan, combine the grits, 1 cup of water, the butter, salt, and a few twists of pepper and bring to a boil. Reduce the heat and cook, stirring occasionally, for 5 to 10 minutes, until thickened to your desired consistency (it will be soupier but edible after 5 minutes, and slightly drier and thicker after 10).

Stir in the spinach and the cheese and cook for 1 minute more, just until the spinach has wilted. Use a large spoon to make a small well in the center of the grits. Crack the egg(s) into a small cup, then drop them into the well. Cover and let the egg(s) and grits cook for 2 to 3 minutes more for a runny yolk or 3 to 4 minutes more for a slightly more set—but still jammy—yolk. Serve with hot sauce, if desired.

MAKE IT IN A RICE COOKER: In a 2-cup capacity rice cooker, whisk the grits, 1¼ cups water, salt, and a few twists of pepper. Cover and turn the rice cooker to the Cook mode. Cook the grits for 15 minutes. Stir, and add the spinach and cheese, cover again, and cook for another 15 minutes. Add the butter and stir until melted. Taste the grits and season with more salt, as desired.

Switch to the Warm mode and use a large spoon to make a small well in the center of the grits. Crack the egg(s) into a small cup, then drop them into the well. Cover and let the egg(s) cook for 2 to 3 minutes for a runny yolk or 3 to 4 minutes for a slightly more set—but still jammy—yolk. Serve with hot sauce, if desired.

SAVORY OATMEAL

Hey guys, I have a message for you from oats: *We're more than just a sweet thing!* Oats are a neutral grain, just as good skewed savory as sweet. A little knob of salted butter and a few turns of the pepper mill is your gateway dish. Then try this one.

SERVES 1

2/3 cup water, broth, or dashi *(Japanese bonito broth)*

Pinch of kosher salt, or 1 teaspoon of miso if you use water

½ cup quick-cooking, gluten-free oats

A drizzle of extra-virgin olive oil or a small knob of unsalted butter

MAKE IT ON THE STOVE: In a small saucepan over medium heat, combine the liquid and the salt or miso (if you're using water) and bring to a lively boil.

Use a wooden spoon to stir in the oats, and reduce the heat to low. Continue to cook, stirring occasionally, for about 5 minutes or until thick. Remove from the heat and stir in the olive oil or butter, and transfer to a bowl.

MAKE IT IN A RICE COOKER: Combine the liquid and the salt or miso (if you're using water) in the rice cooker and heat on the Cook mode, covered, until the water steams, about 3 minutes.

Use a wooden spoon to stir in the oats and continue cooking for 5 minutes more, following the instructions above. Don't wait for the cooker to finish its cycle; just turn it off when the oatmeal is done. Transfer to a bowl and stir in the olive oil or butter

(recipe continues)

NOTE *If you use dashi, it will likely be saltier than standard broth, so you won't need to add much salt (taste and see what you think). If you use a store-bought broth, you'll want a hefty enough pinch of salt, especially if it's low-sodium. If you're using plain old water, adding miso instead of salt will give it the flavor boost it needs.*

Variations

CHEESY OATS: Stir in a teaspoon of spicy mustard and a dash of cayenne with the water or broth (not dashi) and some grated Cheddar cheese in the last minute of cooking. Remove from the heat and stir an egg through the mixture; it will cook in the heat of the oatmeal.

JAPANESE BREAKFAST OATS: Use the dashi in place of water or broth. When the oats are finished cooking, top with a drizzle of toasted sesame oil, a soft- or hard-boiled egg, a piece of nori or a seaweed snack, and some chopped scallions.

HANGOVER HELPER OATS (*#justsaying*): Use chicken broth in place of the water. When the oats are done cooking, top with a soft- or hard-boiled egg, and some crispy garlic chili oil. Keep a big glass of water nearby while you're at it.

HURRY CURRY OATS: Add 1 teaspoon of curry powder to the liquid along with the salt. When the oats are finished cooking, top with cooked chickpeas, yogurt, and Sweet Tomato Chutney (page 148).

BANANA BREAD GRANOLA

DF **VE**

Having trouble making friends? The sweet smell of this granola wafting through the halls will have them swarming around you like flies to honey. I don't advocate bribery but it wouldn't be a bad idea to bring some to your professors.

MAKES 2¼ CUPS

1½ tablespoons melted coconut oil

1 small, extra-ripe banana *(the gnarlier the better)*

1 teaspoon vanilla extract

Pinch of kosher salt

2 tablespoons maple syrup, agave, or honey

1 cup regular *(not quick-cooking)* rolled oats

½ teaspoon ground cinnamon

¼ teaspoon ground cardamom

2 tablespoons chia seeds *(black or white)*

½ cup raw, unsalted pecan pieces

Milk or yogurt, for serving *(optional)*

Preheat the oven to 300°F and line an ⅛-size sheet pan (or the tray from your toaster oven) with a silicone pan liner or nonstick foil.

In a large bowl, combine the coconut oil, banana, vanilla, salt, and maple syrup and stir together with a wooden spoon. Add the oats, cinnamon, cardamom, chia seeds, and pecan pieces. Use your hands (go for it—it's a much better way to make sure all the ingredients are evenly coated!) to toss everything together in the bowl until combined. Spread the granola onto the sheet pan and bake, stirring once halfway through, for 45 to 50 minutes, or until nicely browned and fragrant.

Let cool completely before serving; it will crisp up once it's completely cooled. Store in an airtight container at room temperature for up to a week. Serve with milk or yogurt, if desired.

WAFFLE IRON EGGY TOAST

Here's another one that can go sweet or savory. If you're able to have a waffle iron in your kitchen, this French toast–waffle hybrid is one of the most fun ways to use it. It's best made with good, day-old (or older) challah or soft white bread. The dulce de leche sauce will make this sweeter than the regular sugar will, so opt for that if you're into sweet breakfasts.

SERVES 1

1 tablespoon unsalted butter, at room temperature

1 slice day-old sandwich bread or egg-based bread *(such as challah)*

1 large egg

1 tablespoon milk

Pinch of kosher salt

1 teaspoon sugar or Dulce de Leche *(page 133)*, optional

Nonstick cooking spray

Maple syrup, sliced bananas, or berries, for serving

Preheat the waffle iron and spread the butter on both sides of the bread.

In a shallow bowl, whisk the egg, milk, salt, and sugar (if using) until smooth. Place the bread in the egg mixture for 1 to 2 minutes, then turn it over and set aside until all of the egg mixture is soaked up, about 2 minutes more. (You can also soak the bread overnight in the fridge, especially if it's on the stale side.)

When the waffle iron is hot, spray it with the nonstick spray and place the eggy bread on the bottom side. Close the lid and cook for 2 to 3 minutes, or until the bread is nicely browned. (Feel free to lift the lid to peek at it.) Transfer the waffle-toast to a plate and serve with some good maple syrup and sliced bananas or fresh berries.

Variations

CRÈME BRÛLÉE: Combine 1 tablespoon sugar and ¼ teaspoon cinnamon, and stir this into the butter before spreading onto the bread. Add a little splash of vanilla extract to the egg mixture and follow the directions above.

LEMON CUSTARD: Add 1 teaspoon freshly grated lemon zest (the lemon's skin) and a little splash of vanilla extract to the egg mixture. Follow the directions above.

SAVORY PEPPER-PARM: Omit the sugar from the egg mixture. Stir 1 tablespoon of grated Parmesan cheese into the butter before spreading onto the bread, and add a few good turns of the pepper mill to the egg mixture. Follow the directions above.

GOOD

GRAINS

TO KEEP YOU GOING

"CHEATERS NEVER PROSPER"

BAKED RAVIOLI LASAGNE

Oh yes they do. Think of this as Cliffs Notes for lasagne. Ravioli already has the filling and the pasta sheets, and if you do it this way you won't even have to boil the pasta first. I like spinach and cheese ravioli but you could use any flavor you fancy. (Mushroom! Mushroom is good, too.)

SERVES 3 TO 4

Nonstick cooking spray

1½ cups Core Tomato Sauce *(page 147),* or your favorite store-bought tomato sauce

1 *(9-ounce)* package fresh ravioli

½ cup grated mozzarella, plus more as desired

½ cup grated pecorino Romano or Parmesan cheese

MAKE IT IN THE OVEN: Preheat the oven or toaster oven to 350°F. Spray a 6 × 8-inch oven-safe baking dish with nonstick cooking spray.

Spread ½ cup of the tomato sauce on the bottom of the baking dish, then arrange half of the ravioli on top of the sauce. Spread an additional ½ cup tomato sauce, ¼ cup of the mozzarella, and ¼ cup of the pecorino on top of the ravioli. Repeat this process with the remaining ravioli, the remaining ½ cup tomato sauce, and the remaining cheese, ending with the pecorino. Top with some additional mozzarella, if you like it extra cheesy.

Cover the dish with nonstick foil (or foil sprayed with nonstick cooking spray, so it doesn't stick to the cheese). Bake for 45 minutes, then uncover and continue to bake until the sauce is bubbly

and the cheese is nice and browned, about 15 minutes more.

Remove the lasagne from the oven and let sit for about 15 minutes, loosely covered with the foil, before serving.

MAKE IT IN A RICE COOKER: If your rice cooker has a capacity of 6 cups or more, you can make the full recipe. Otherwise, make half. *#mathskillsatwork*

Heat the rice cooker on the Cook mode. Follow the recipe above, but add ¼ cup of water to the tomato sauce before you start assembling directly in the rice cooker. Once the lasagne is assembled, cover the rice cooker with the lid instead of foil and bake for 20 minutes (for half of the recipe) to 30 minutes (for the full recipe), until the lasagne is bubbly and heated through.

Turn off the heat and let the lasagne sit in the rice cooker, covered, for 10 to 15 minutes more, before serving. (You can keep it on the Warm setting for up to an hour if you're not quite ready to eat.)

ONE-POT SPAGHETTI
CACIO E PEPE

Say it with me and don't pronounce the "i" in "cacio"!: "KAH-cho ey PE-pey." In Italy, an *americanata* is anything crazy and borderline genius thought up and acted on by an American. Wanna freak out an Italian? Tell them you made one of their most traditional pasta dishes *in one pot.* #Americanata

SERVES 4

1 garlic clove, chopped

2 teaspoons kosher salt

1 teaspoon freshly ground black pepper

3 tablespoons extra-virgin olive oil

3 cups boiling water

½ pound spaghetti

½ cup grated pecorino Romano or Parmesan cheese

MAKE IT ON THE STOVE: In a large saucepan over high heat, combine the garlic, salt, pepper, olive oil, and the boiling water and bring to a boil (the water will still be hot, but it will need to come back to a boil once everything has been added). Break the spaghetti in half and add it to the pot, stirring to prevent clumping. Turn the heat down so the liquid bubbles gently, cover, and let cook for 5 minutes. Stir the pasta again to help it soak up some of the liquid, cover again, and continue to cook for 3 minutes more.

Uncover the pasta and continue to cook about 4 minutes more, until the spaghetti is al dente (i.e., still has a bit of a bite to it) and most of the liquid has been soaked up. Remove the saucepan from the heat, add the cheese, and

stir to coat the spaghetti evenly. The remaining few tablespoons of liquid will combine with the cheese to make a light sauce that just coats the pasta.

MAKE IT IN A RICE COOKER: Set your rice cooker to Cook mode. Add the garlic, salt, pepper, olive oil, and boiling water, cover, and bring back to a boil.

Break the spaghetti in half and add it to the pot, stirring as much as possible to prevent clumping. Cover and let cook for 5 minutes. Stir the pasta again to help it soak up some of the liquid, cover again, and cook for 3 minutes more.

Uncover the pasta and continue to cook about 4 minutes more, until the spaghetti is al dente (i.e., still has a bit of a bite to it) and most of the liquid has been soaked up. Turn off the heat, add the cheese, and stir to coat the spaghetti evenly. The remaining few tablespoons of liquid will combine with the cheese to make a light sauce that just coats the pasta.

ONE-POT PASTA

WITH SAUSAGE & BROCCOLI

About prepping that broccoli: *Eat the stalks!* Just peel away the tough skin with a paring knife or vegetable peeler and chop the stalks into pieces. There's almost as much stalk as floret in a bunch of broccoli and it tastes just like . . . broccoli. So eat it.

SERVES 4

1½ cups boiling water

1 cup Core Tomato Sauce *(page 147)*, or your favorite store-bought tomato sauce

1 teaspoon kosher salt

2 cooked sausages *(such as Italian chicken sausage)*, about 4 ounces each, sliced

2 garlic cloves, chopped

2 tablespoons extra-virgin olive oil

1½ cups fusilli, or any other short pasta

1 cup chopped broccoli

Grated Parmesan cheese, for serving

Red pepper flakes, for serving *(optional)*

MAKE IT ON THE STOVE: In a large saucepan over medium heat, combine the boiling water, tomato sauce, salt, sausages, garlic, olive oil, and fusilli. Bring back to a boil, cover, and cook for 5 minutes.

Uncover the saucepan to stir everything together once more, cover again, and cook for 5 minutes more. Add the broccoli and continue to cook, uncovered, stirring occasionally, until the pasta is al dente (i.e., still has a bit of bite to it) and the broccoli is fork-tender, about 4 to 5 minutes more. Stir in the Parmesan and red pepper flakes, as desired.

MAKE IT IN A RICE COOKER: Set your rice cooker to Cook mode. Add the boiling water, tomato sauce, salt, sausages, garlic, and olive oil and bring back to a boil.

When the water is boiling, add the pasta, stir, and cook, covered, for 5 minutes. Uncover the rice cooker to give everything a stir, cover again, and cook for 5 minutes more. Add the broccoli and continue to cook, uncovered, stirring occasionally, until the pasta is al dente (i.e., still has a bit of bite to it) and the broccoli is fork-tender, about 4 to 5 minutes more. Stir in the Parmesan and red pepper flakes, as desired.

TIP *Make it GF by using GF pasta; make it vegetarian by using vegetarian "sausage" and/or make it vegan by omitting the cheese.*

ONE-POT PASTA
WITH CHICKPEAS

This is the one that went viral after Food52 named it a Genius Recipe. It seems incredibly simple at first, but it is indeed a *#geniusrecipe*. If you have a cheese shop or an Italian deli nearby, see if they'll give you a piece of a Parmesan rind (the tough outer "skin" of the original wheel of cheese). Cooked with sauces or soups, the rind gives you all the flavor of Parmesan (or any similar hard cheese, such as pecorino Romano) for virtually no cost.

SERVES 2

¼ cup extra-virgin olive oil

4 garlic cloves, smashed

¼ cup tomato paste

2 teaspoons kosher salt

1 *(15-ounce)* can chickpeas, drained

1 cup small pasta, such as ditalini, shells, or elbows

3 cups boiling water

Grated Parmesan or pecorino Romano cheese, for serving

Red pepper flakes, for serving *(optional)*

NOTE *If you have a teakettle (electric or otherwise), go ahead and use that to boil the 3 cups of water in the ingredients so that it's ready to go for that second step.*

In a large saucepan, heat the olive oil over medium heat. Add the garlic and cook, stirring occasionally, until the garlic starts to brown and becomes fragrant, about 3 minutes.

Add the tomato paste and salt (carefully, as the tomato paste might spatter) and cook, stirring, for just 1 minute. Add the chickpeas, pasta, and the boiling water. Bring it to a gentle boil, then cover and cook for 15 to 20 minutes, stirring halfway through, or until the pasta is al dente (still with a bit of bite to it) and most of the liquid has been absorbed. You'll end up with just enough sauce to coat the pasta and chickpeas.

Add the cheese and red pepper flakes as desired and stir to incorporate. Serve hot.

BLACK BEANS & RICE

Go to any Cuban diner and you'll see these black beans and rice on the menu—often referred to as Moros y Cristianos (meaning Moors and Christians, referring to the Moors who once occupied the Iberian peninsula and the Christian Iberians who in turn occupied Cuba). It's an incredibly yummy and versatile dish and can be topped with anything you please.

SERVES 4 TO 6

1 cup long-grain white rice

1 (15-ounce) can black beans

SOFRITO

3 tablespoons extra-virgin olive oil

1 medium onion, chopped

1 small green or red bell pepper, stemmed, seeded, and chopped

2 garlic cloves, chopped

1 tablespoon tomato paste

½ teaspoon dried oregano

1 teaspoon ground cumin

1 bay leaf

1½ teaspoons kosher salt

Freshly ground black pepper

Pickled Tink Onions (page 150), for serving (optional)

Pour the rice into a fine-mesh strainer and run it under cold water, swishing the rice with your hands, until the water runs clear. (This removes most of the starch from the rice, which can otherwise make it sticky.) Let it drain over the sink or over a medium bowl and set aside. Drain the can of black beans and set aside as well.

Meanwhile, make the sofrito. Heat the olive oil in a large shallow saucepan with a tight-fitting lid over medium-high heat until it shimmers. Add the onion, bell pepper, and garlic and cook, stirring occasionally, until everything has softened and is beginning to brown, about 5 minutes. Add the tomato paste, oregano, cumin, and bay leaf and stir to combine. Cook about 1 minute more, or until the mixture is fragrant. Stir in the salt and pepper.

(recipe continues)

TIP *When buying tomato paste, try to buy it in a tube rather than a can—the tube is much easier to keep in the fridge for longer (it will last for 1 month after opening).*

Add the black beans and 2 cups of water and bring to a boil. Add the rice and bring to a boil again. Cover the saucepan, reduce the heat to a gentle simmer, and cook until all of the liquid has been absorbed, about 25 minutes. (Leave it alone while it's cooking. Don't lift the lid or stir it; just be patient.)

Remove the saucepan from the heat and let the rice and beans rest for 15 minutes before serving. Remove the bay leaf. Top with the Pickled Tink Onions, if you'd like.

Variations

LEBANESE LENTILS, RICE, AND CRISPY ONIONS: Rinse the rice just as in the recipe above. In place of the sofrito, heat 2 tablespoons of extra-virgin olive oil over medium-high heat and add 1 large onion, thinly sliced, and cook until it starts to soften, about 5 minutes. Reduce the heat and continue to cook, stirring frequently, until the onion has become very soft and is beginning to caramelize, 10 to 15 minutes more.

Add 1 teaspoon ground cumin, ½ teaspoon ground cinnamon, and 1 bay leaf and season with 1½ teaspoons kosher salt and a few good turns of the pepper mill. Add 1 (15-ounce) can of lentils, drained, and 2 cups of water or broth. Bring to a boil, then add the rice and continue as in the above recipe.

To serve, stir a handful of freshly torn mint leaves into the rice mixture and divide among several bowls. Top each bowl with store-bought crispy fried onions (the kind that go on top of green bean casserole!).

RED BEANS AND COCONUT RICE, THE BELIZEAN WAY: Make the sofrito as in the original recipe, but use 2 tablespoons coconut oil instead of the olive oil and use 3 cloves of garlic rather than 2. Add 1½ teaspoons dried thyme instead of the oregano when adding the herbs and spices.

Use 1 (15-ounce) can of red beans or red kidney beans in place of the black beans, and add 2 cups of coconut water to the saucepan rather than regular water. Stir in a handful of chopped cilantro just before serving.

BANG BANG CHICKEN & RICE NOODLES

The crazy thing about this is that you can make the whole entire thing with an electric teakettle! The name comes from the sound your hammer or rolling pin makes when you bash the chicken to turn it into shreds.

SERVES 2

3 slices fresh ginger, cut into coins

1 scallion, white and light green parts only

1 teaspoon kosher salt

1 boneless, skinless chicken breast *(about 5 ounces)*

1 (3¾-ounce) bag rice noodles *(or cellophane noodles or bean threads)*

Half of a cucumber, peeled, seeded, and cut into thin strips

Bang Bang Sauce *(page 144)*

Toasted sesame seeds and fresh cilantro, for serving

MAKE IT ON THE STOVE: In a small saucepan, combine the ginger, scallion, salt, and 2 cups of water over medium-high heat and bring to a boil. Add the chicken and when it returns to a boil, reduce the heat to low, cover, and let the chicken simmer gently for 30 minutes.

When the chicken is cooked through (cut into it a bit to make sure it's no longer pink), remove the chicken from the saucepan and transfer it to a reusable zipper storage bag, but don't seal it completely. Discard the ginger and scallion, reserving the liquid.

Add the rice noodles to the hot broth in the saucepan. They will cook in the heat of the liquid in about 7 minutes.

Meanwhile, use a rolling pin or a small hammer to pound ("bang bang") the chicken until it falls apart in shreds. Combine the chicken with the cucumber in a medium bowl and toss with half of the Bang Bang Sauce.

Drain the noodles and divide them equally between two bowls. Top with the chicken and cucumber and garnish with the sesame seeds and cilantro. Serve with the remaining sauce on the side.

MAKE IT IN AN ELECTRIC TEAKETTLE: Combine the ginger, scallion, salt, chicken, and 1 cup water in a reusable zipper storage bag and seal it well.

Fill the kettle half-full with water, lower the zipper bag with the chicken into the water so that it's totally submerged, and bring to a boil. Once the teakettle has reached a boil and turned itself off, keep the bag in the kettle to allow the chicken to cook (in the residual heat) for 10 minutes. Repeat this process twice more by switching the kettle back on so that it boils again, and leaving the chicken in the kettle for 10 minutes each time, for 30 minutes total. Check to make sure the chicken is cooked through by cutting into it to make sure it's firm and no longer pink inside.

Divide the noodles between two bowls and pour the broth from the zipper bag over them, discarding the ginger and garlic. The noodles will cook in the heat of the liquid. Leave the chicken in the bag, and use a rolling pin or a small hammer to pound ("bang bang") the chicken until it falls apart in shreds. Proceed as in the recipe above.

NOTE *You can poach fish with the same method. Check to see if it's cooked after the first 10 minutes; fish cooks much faster than chicken.*

RICE, RICE, BABY

Rice is the staple food of over half the world's population, and not just because it's cheap. Rice tastes good and powers you *up*. It can be a tricky thing to cook, though. So follow these recipes and use a heavy-bottomed pot with a tight-fitting lid. Or an electric rice cooker (recommended). Any leftovers can become a Crispy Rice Cake (see Variations) the next day.

SERVES 2

1 cup sushi rice

In a large bowl, combine the rice with 1½ cups cold water. Use your hands to mix together and carefully pour the water out. Repeat this 2 or 3 more times, until the water is nearly clear. Cover the rice with 1½ cups fresh water and let it soak for 30 minutes.

Transfer the rice and water to a heavy-bottomed pot with a lid and bring to a boil, uncovered. Stir once and reduce the heat to low, then cover and cook at the lowest possible heat for 15 minutes. (No peeking!) Turn off the heat and let the rice stand for 15 minutes before serving.

Variations

BASMATI RICE: Use basmati rice and 1¾ cups water, and a generous pinch of kosher salt. (Best served with a knob of salted butter stirred in after cooking.)

LONG-GRAIN WHITE RICE: Wash, but don't soak, 1 cup rice in a fine-mesh sieve, rinsing until the water runs clear. Combine the rice with 2 cups water and a generous pinch of kosher salt in a heavy-bottomed pot. Let the rice simmer uncovered until you start to see it peeking up through the water, then cover, turn the heat down as low as it will go, and proceed as in the above recipe.

(recipe continues)

More Variations

SOBORO BEEF OR CHICKEN: In a large skillet over medium heat, brown ½ pound lean ground beef or chicken, breaking it up with a wooden spoon into small crumbles. Cook for 8 to 10 minutes, stirring occasionally, until the meat has browned nicely and is no longer pink. Add 1 tablespoon of tamari or soy sauce, 1 tablespoon mirin, 1 tablespoon sugar, 1 teaspoon freshly grated ginger, and 2 tablespoons water. Cook, stirring frequently, until the liquid is absorbed, about 8 minutes. Serve on top of the rice and mix in some cooked peas. Top with freshly chopped herbs, such as cilantro or parsley, as well as the Pickled Tink Onions (page 54), if you like.

BRAIN FOOD AND MAYO: Drain a can of tuna, salmon, shrimp, mussels, sardines, or (my favorite) smoked oysters. Combine the fish in a small bowl with a few tablespoons of mayonnaise and a squirt of sriracha and serve alongside the rice.

FRIED EGG AND CRISPY GARLIC CHILI OIL: Just like it sounds: Fry an egg or cook it any way you like (try the Teakettle Eggs on page 151). Top it with a good slog of chili oil and serve on top of the rice. A few chopped scallions or a handful of spinach stirred into the hot rice wouldn't be out of place.

CRISPY RICE CAKE: This is best with cold leftover sushi rice. Other rice may not stick together to form a cake but it'll still be crispy. Anyway: In a small nonstick skillet over medium heat, heat 1 tablespoon vegetable oil or sesame oil until it shimmers. Add about 1 cup of leftover rice, pressing it down with a spatula or large spoon to flatten it into a circle. Cook until the rice starts to sizzle and the bottom of the cake has become crispy, about 8 to 10 minutes (check by lifting up a corner of the rice with a silicone spatula). Flip the rice over with a silicone spatula (it may hold together but it may not—don't stress). Pour another tablespoon of oil around the edges of the rice and cook for about 5 minutes more, until the oil has been absorbed and the underside of the rice has crisped up. In a separate skillet over high heat, fry a slice of bacon until crisp. Add an egg, and scramble them together, breaking up the bacon with the spatula. Plop the bacon and egg on top of the rice with a squirt of ketchup to settle an upset tummy on a Sunday morning.

COUSCOUS & VEGGIES

WITH SPICED BROTH

Couscous is one of those "neutral" grains you should always have around. (Well, it isn't technically a grain—it's semolina rubbed together with droplets of water to form delicious little pellets of something that looks, tastes, and acts like a grain but isn't.) Couscous refers to both the grain itself and dishes that are served with it. The grain can skew sweet or savory and takes just a few minutes to prepare. I love it for breakfast with cinnamon, date sugar, and coconut milk, as well as in this super simple riff on a traditional Moroccan dish called seven-vegetable couscous. If you want to scale this down slightly for fewer than four people, you can simply use less vegetables (anywhere from 1 to 2 cups).

SERVES 4

1 bunch of cilantro

1 tablespoon extra-virgin olive oil

1 medium yellow onion, chopped

1 teaspoon ground ginger

1 teaspoon ground turmeric

¼ teaspoon ground cinnamon

1 cup diced tomatoes, fresh or canned

1 quart vegetable or chicken broth

1½ teaspoons kosher salt

Freshly ground black pepper

1 (15-ounce) can chickpeas, drained and rinsed

3 cups of mixed vegetables, such as cabbage, zucchini, carrots, turnips, sweet potato, and/or butternut or acorn squash, peeled and cut in large chunks

1½ cups couscous

Raisins or golden raisins (optional)

MAKE IT ON THE STOVE: Divide the bunch of cilantro in two and tie one half of the bunch together with a piece of kitchen string. Chop the remaining cilantro (no need to separate stems and leaves), and set aside.

In a large saucepan over medium heat, heat the olive oil until it shimmers. Add the onion and cook until it has softened and is just beginning to brown, about 5 minutes. Add the ginger, turmeric, cinnamon, tomatoes, broth, and the tied bunch of cilantro and season with the salt and a few good turns of the pepper mill. Bring to a boil, then reduce the heat to low and simmer gently for 15 minutes.

(recipe continues)

Add the chickpeas and the cabbage and root vegetables (omit the zucchini for now, if using at all) and simmer, covered, for 10 to 20 minutes more, or until the vegetables are tender when pierced with a fork. (If you are using zucchini, add it now and let the mixture cook for 5 minutes more.)

Meanwhile, combine the couscous and raisins (if using) in a serving bowl.

When the vegetables are fork-tender, remove and discard the half-bunch of cilantro. Use a ladle to scoop 1 cup of the broth into a heatproof measuring cup. Pour it over the couscous, and immediately cover with a plate or foil to allow the couscous to absorb the liquid. Let sit 5 minutes.

Uncover the serving bowl and fluff the couscous with a fork to gently separate the grains. Transfer the rest of the broth and the veggies to the serving bowl on top of the couscous, and top everything with the reserved chopped cilantro.

MAKE IT IN A RICE COOKER: Make sure your rice cooker has a capacity of at least 6 cups, and use only half of the recipe above.

Set your rice cooker to Cook mode and proceed with the recipe above, but omit the olive oil.

MAKE IT IN A SLOW COOKER: As long as your slow cooker has a capacity of 2 quarts, you can make the full recipe.

Turn the slow cooker to High and follow the directions for cooking on the stove, omitting the olive oil. It will take 1 hour to cook the broth with the tomatoes and spices, 35 to 40 minutes to cook the chickpeas and root vegetables, and 5 to 10 minutes to cook the zucchini.

OMURICE ("OMELET RICE")

Fun fact: There are nearly 140,000 posts with the hashtag _#omurice_. Why? Omurice is a staple of Japanese home cooking and it is simply perfection. Crispy rice; salty, sweet, and tangy caramelization; bits of juicy chicken or bacon; and enough vegetables to make you feel virtuous, all wrapped up in eggs—fried on one side and creamy on the other—then drizzled with ketchup. What's not to love? It's a fine repository for leftover cooked vegetables, too.

SERVES 1

2 teaspoons
vegetable oil

Half of a small onion
or two scallions
*(light green part
only)*, chopped

1 boneless, skinless
chicken thigh or half
of a boneless, skinless
chicken breast, diced

¼ bell pepper,
seeded and chopped
(any kind)

A few mushrooms,
cleaned, trimmed,
and chopped

Pinch of kosher salt

¼ teaspoon ground
white pepper, or freshly
ground black pepper,
to taste

½ cup fresh or leftover
cooked rice

2 to 3 tablespoons
ketchup, plus more
for serving

2 large eggs, whisked
together with
1 tablespoon water

In a small nonstick skillet, heat 1 teaspoon of the oil over medium-high heat until it shimmers. Add the onion and cook, stirring occasionally, for about 2 minutes, or until it has started to soften.

Add the chicken, bell pepper, and mushrooms, and continue to cook for 2 to 4 minutes more,

stirring occasionally, until the chicken is no longer pink and the vegetables are starting to turn brown. Reduce the heat to medium and season generously with salt and pepper. (Don't be afraid to go a little overboard if you're adding unsalted rice.) Gently stir the rice into the chicken mixture in the skillet.

With a silicone spatula, push some of the rice aside so you can squirt the ketchup right into the hot pan. When the ketchup sizzles (this happens fast), quickly stir it into the rice. Remove the rice mixture from the pan and set aside, covered, to keep warm.

Wipe out the skillet and return it to medium heat with the remaining 1 teaspoon of oil. When the oil is shimmering, add the beaten eggs and swirl the pan so that the eggs cover the bottom. Let cook for a few seconds and quickly lift the cooked edge of the eggs to let the uncooked egg run under. Do this all the way around. When the bottom is cooked (use a spatula to peek at the underside) but the top is still runny, add the rice back to the skillet and let it cook with the eggs for about 1 minute more.

Remove the skillet from the heat and, with a plate nearby, carefully flip the mixture over so the egg/omelet is on top and the rice is on the bottom. Use the spatula to tuck two edges of the egg under the rice so it looks like a roll, or find someone to show you the fancy way. Serve with additional ketchup.

MEAT & NON-MEAT

TO FEED A CROWD

(OR JUST YOUR ROOMMATES)

CHEESEBOARD SCHEMATIC

~~~~~~~~

If the cutting board with which you've outfitted your *petite cuisine* is wooden, you're halfway to a cheeseboard. What we're after is nothing more than a nice wooden board upon which you will create an artful but not pretentious arrangement of nibbly bits for as many friends as you care to entertain. It'll take five minutes—four and a half of which you'll spend unwrapping things. #IMHO, every successful cheeseboard starts with the same formula: something cheesy, meaty, sweet, savory, fruity, and crunchy. On the following pages are some tips and a little schematic to get you started.

	CHEESY	MEATY	SWEET	SAVORY	FRUITY	CRUNCHY
ITALIAN	Parmesan	Pepperoni	Dried Figs	Black Olives	Green Grapes	Crostini
SPANISH	Manchego	Chorizo	Dates	Roasted Almonds	Apples	Baguette
ENGLISH	Cheddar	Ham	Tomato Chutney	Pecans	Pears	Whole Wheat Crackers
FRENCH	Brie	Prosciutto	Honey	Honey-Roasted Walnuts	Pomegranate (seeds or fruit, halved)	Water Crackers
	Goat	Hard Salami	Dried Cherries	Pistachios	Tangerines	Buttery Crackers
DANISH	Blue	Speck	Dried Cranberries	Cornichons	Red Grapes	Ridged Potato Chips
GREEK	Feta	Beef Jerky	Apricot Jam	Sun-Dried Tomatoes	Strawberries	Sweet Potato Chips
		Linguiça	Orange Marmalade	Green Olives		Pita Chips
			Mango Chutney	Peppadew Peppers		Flatbread
						Pretzels

QUICK AND EASY FORMULAS

1. Parmesan, prosciutto, soppressata, dried figs, fig jam, green olives, red grapes, crostini, salted peanuts

2. Manchego, chorizo, beef jerky, dates, honey, roasted almonds, tangerines, sesame flatbread

3. Cheddar, Black Forest ham, tomato chutney (see page 148), pecans, apples, whole wheat crackers, mustard pretzels

4. Brie, speck, summer sausage, orange marmalade, strawberries, walnuts, baguette, sweet potato and beet chips

5. Goat cheese, Genoa salami, sun-dried tomatoes, Peppadew peppers, cornichons, red grapes, black pepper crackers

6. Blue cheese, hard salami, dried cranberries, honey-roasted walnuts, pears, buttery crackers

7. Feta, linguiça, dried apricots, kalamata olives, pistachios, pomegranate, pita chips

CHEESEBALLS ALL DAY

There's gotta be a better name for these creamy, cheesy, more-ish little balls of deliciousness. (Cheese Spheres? Cheese Globes? Balls of Deliciousness?) If a cheeseboard is too much of a commitment of artistry or expense, then the cheeseball's for you. Start with a base of butter and cheese, then use your imagination; and make sure you have plenty of crackers or your dipping accessory of choice for serving the finished product. There are a zillion ways you can tweak it. Here are four.

EACH MAKES ONE 4-INCH CHEESEBALL

VG PIMENTO CHEESEBALL

4 tablespoons (½ stick) salted butter, at room temperature

1 (8-ounce) package cream cheese, at room temperature

1½ cups (6 ounces) freshly shredded sharp Cheddar cheese

¼ teaspoon cayenne

½ cup crushed cheese crackers (such as Cheez-Its) or cheese puffs

In a medium bowl, use a wooden spoon (and plenty of elbow grease!) to beat the butter and cream cheese until blended, but not too vigorously or the cheeseball will deflate. Then beat in the Cheddar and cayenne.

Wrap into a ball in plastic wrap and refrigerate at least 2 hours, until firm. Then unwrap it and roll in the crushed cheese crackers just before serving.

CHEESEBALL GAUDÍ

4 tablespoons (½ stick) salted butter, at room temperature

1 (8-ounce) package cream cheese, at room temperature

1 cup (4 ounces) freshly grated manchego cheese

½ to 1 teaspoon smoked paprika

¼ teaspoon cayenne

6 green olives, pitted and chopped

½ cup chopped roasted, salted almonds

In a medium bowl, use a wooden spoon to beat the butter and cream cheese until blended. Add the manchego, paprika, and cayenne and continue to beat, but not too vigorously or the cheeseball will deflate. Use a silicone spatula to gently stir in the olives.

Form the mixture into a ball in plastic wrap and refrigerate at least 2 hours, until firm. Unwrap and roll in the chopped almonds just before serving.

VEG OUT CHEESEBALL

4 tablespoons (½ stick) salted butter, at room temperature

1 (8-ounce) package cream cheese, at room temperature

1 cup (4 ounces) freshly grated white Cheddar cheese

2 to 3 tablespoons Hidden Valley Ranch seasoning mix

1 scallion (white and green parts only), chopped

2 tablespoons chopped red bell pepper

1 cup shredded carrot

In a medium bowl, use a wooden spoon to beat together the butter and cream cheese until blended. Add the Cheddar and stir to combine, but not too vigorously or the cheeseball will deflate. Stir in the ranch seasoning, scallion, bell pepper, and ½ cup of the shredded carrot.

Wrap into a ball in plastic wrap and refrigerate for about 2 hours, until firm. Unwrap the cheese ball and roll in the remaining ½ cup shredded carrot just before serving.

BIRTHDAY CAKE CHEESEBALL

4 tablespoons (½ stick) unsalted butter, at room temperature

2 (8-ounce) packages cream cheese, at room temperature

⅓ cup powdered sugar

¾ cup store-bought yellow cake mix

½ cup rainbow sprinkles

In a medium bowl, use a wooden spoon to beat together the butter and cream cheese until blended. Add the powdered sugar and the cake mix and stir to combine, but not too vigorously or the cheeseball will deflate.

Wrap into a ball in plastic wrap and refrigerate for about 2 hours, or until firm. Unwrap the ball and roll in the sprinkles just before serving.

SECRET-INGREDIENT CRISPY BAKED
CHICKEN CUTLETS

You definitely don't need one of those fancy air fryer contraptions to get your fried chicken fix. This chicken's got all the crunch of fried chicken but it's *baked*. The mayo keeps it juicy and the cornflakes make it crunchy. Switch it up by rubbing different herbs or spices (lemon zest and rosemary, anyone?) into the chicken with the salt and pepper, or keep it simple.

SERVES 2

¼ cup cornflakes

2 boneless, skinless chicken breasts (about 5 ounces each)

Kosher salt

½ teaspoon freshly ground black pepper

¼ cup mayonnaise

½ teaspoon garlic powder, or 1 small clove of garlic, finely chopped

3 tablespoons grated Parmesan cheese

Pour the cornflakes into a sealable zipper bag and close the seal. Crunch the bag in your hands until the cornflakes are the size of bread crumbs. A few larger pieces are fine.

Preheat the oven or toaster oven to 425°F. Line an ⅛-size sheet pan with nonstick foil. Rub both sides of the chicken with salt—start with a few pinches and make sure the chicken is covered in salt allllll the way around the sides—and do the same with the pepper. Set the chicken on the sheet pan and set aside.

In a small bowl or cup, use a spoon to combine the mayonnaise, garlic powder, and Parmesan. Use your hands to slather the mayonnaise mixture all over the chicken and make sure the top and sides of the chicken are fully coated.

Transfer the chicken back to the sheet pan and sprinkle the cornflakes on top. Use your hands to press them gently into the mayo coat.

Bake for 15 to 20 minutes, until the chicken is cooked through (you can cut each piece in the middle to make sure it's no longer pink) and the cornflake crust is deep golden brown and crispy.

CHICKEN ADOBO

This isn't the sexiest-looking chicken, but it's easy and has a great personality. And it's even better the next day. Adobo is the kind of thing to make when you crave big, bold flavors and a hug. Serve it in a bowl with white rice to sop up all the delicious juices.

SERVES 3 TO 4

2 tablespoons extra-virgin olive oil

2 pounds bone-in, skin-on chicken thighs and/or legs *(about 6 pieces)*

5 large garlic cloves

2 bay leaves

½ cup distilled white vinegar

½ cup tamari or soy sauce

½ to 1 teaspoon freshly ground black pepper

Steamed rice, for serving *(see page 52)*

MAKE IT ON THE STOVE: In a large saucepan with a lid, heat the olive oil over medium-high heat until it shimmers. Add the chicken, skin side down, and cook for 5 minutes on each side, until browned. Add the garlic and let it sizzle for a minute, then add the bay leaves, vinegar, tamari, black pepper, and 1 cup of water. Bring the mixture to a boil, then reduce the heat to low, cover, and let simmer for 30 minutes, turning the chicken over halfway through cooking.

Uncover the saucepan, increase the heat to medium-high, and let the mixture continue to cook at a boil for 15 to 20 minutes, until the liquid has reduced and thickened so that there's just enough sauce to coat the chicken.

Remove and discard the bay leaves. Serve the chicken and the adobo sauce over steamed rice.

MAKE IT IN A SLOW COOKER: Combine the chicken, garlic, bay leaves, vinegar, tamari, black pepper, and 1 cup of water in a slow cooker. Cook on High for 3 hours or on Low for 6 hours.

Remove the bay leaves. Serve the chicken and the adobo sauce over steamed rice.

Variation

PORK BELLY ADOBO: Substitute 2 pounds of pork belly for the chicken and cook, covered, for 1½ hours, then uncovered for about 30 minutes more. This is extra good if you refrigerate the pork adobo overnight after it finishes cooking. To reheat, remove the meat from the liquid, cut it into large chunks, and brown it in a skillet on both sides, using the solidified fat from the top. Reheat the liquid separately in a saucepan or the microwave and serve, along with the meat, over steamed rice.

PIRI PIRI CHICKEN LOLLIPOPS

Okay, so they're drumsticks, not lollipops. If you want to get fancy, use your paring knife to push the skin up from the "handle," scraping it free from the bone. When it's cooked, all the meat will gather up at the top in a nice little . . . well . . . *lollipop*, making it easy to pick up with your hands and chomp. Make double the amount of the piri piri sauce. It'll be the hot sauce you put on ev-ery-thing.

SERVES 2

4 chicken drumsticks

1 tablespoon extra-virgin olive oil

1 teaspoon kosher salt

Freshly ground black pepper

1/2 cup Piri Piri Sauce *(page 145)*

Preheat the oven to 400°F and line a small sheet pan with nonstick foil.

Rub the drumsticks all over with the oil, salt, and pepper and arrange on the sheet pan. Roast for 10 minutes, flip the drumsticks, and roast for 10 minutes more.

Use a spoon or a silicone brush (if you have one) to coat the drumsticks in half of the piri piri sauce. Return the chicken to the oven for 8 minutes, until the drumsticks are golden brown. Flip the drumsticks again and brush on the remaining sauce. Return the chicken to the oven and roast until very browned and tender, about 8 minutes more.

KEEMA

 GF **DF**

The first time I had keema, it was described as "Indian chili." That's about as broad a comparison as could be. Yes, they both have garlic and onion and spices in common—but not the same spices. They have ground meat in common, unless you're in Texas, in which case they have almost nothing in common. You won't find keema in restaurants; it's Indian home cooking, and despite being super easy to throw together, it has all the complex flavors you want in Indian food. Serve it with naan bread, over rice, wrapped in a warmed flour tortilla, or scooped up with lentil crackers. A fried egg wouldn't be out of place here.

SERVES 3 TO 4

2 tablespoons vegetable oil

1 yellow onion, chopped

2 large garlic cloves, finely chopped

2 teaspoons freshly grated ginger

2 teaspoons garam masala

1 teaspoon ground coriander

¼ teaspoon ground turmeric

1 pound lean ground beef or chicken

1 cup diced tomatoes *(fresh or canned)*

1 teaspoon kosher salt

½ teaspoon freshly ground black pepper

½ cup frozen peas

Handful of fresh cilantro, roughly chopped

Freshly squeezed lime juice, for serving

Sweet Tomato Chutney *(page 148)*, **for serving**

NOTE *Garam masala, a spice blend common in Indian cooking, is very easy to buy online. Infinitely worth it.*

In a large skillet over medium-high heat, heat the oil until it shimmers. Add the onion, garlic, and ginger and cook, stirring occasionally, until the onion has softened and is beginning to brown, 3 to 4 minutes. Add the garam masala, coriander, and turmeric, stirring to incorporate. Add the meat and use a large spoon to break it up into smaller pieces. Cook for 8 to 10 minutes, stirring occasionally, until the meat has browned nicely and is no longer pink.

Add the tomatoes, salt, black pepper, and peas, along with ¼ cup of water. Cook, stirring occasionally to scrape up the browned bits on the bottom of the pan (where all the flavor is), until the peas are tender and most of the liquid is absorbed, 4 to 5 minutes more.

Remove the keema from the heat and top with the cilantro. Divide the keema among bowls, top each serving with a squeeze of lime juice, and serve the Sweet Tomato Chutney alongside.

BOLLYWOOD BUTTER CHICKEN

The name of this über-popular dish is misleading: Butter is a bit player here, with savory, sweet, spicy flavors taking the lead. Make this for your friends when you want something soothing and restorative. It's great with steamed basmati rice and Sweet Tomato Chutney.

SERVES 6

1 cup plain yogurt

1 teaspoon ground turmeric

2 teaspoons garam masala

1 teaspoon ground cumin

¼ teaspoon cayenne

2 teaspoons kosher salt

Juice of 1 lemon

4 boneless, skinless chicken breasts, or 6 boneless, skinless chicken thighs, cut into 1-inch chunks

4 tablespoons (½ stick) unsalted butter

1 large onion, sliced

1 tablespoon freshly grated ginger

4 garlic cloves, chopped

1 teaspoon paprika

½ teaspoon ground cinnamon

1 (28-ounce) can diced tomatoes, with the juice

½ cup heavy cream

Coarsely chopped cilantro, for serving

Steamed basmati rice (page 52), for serving

Sweet Tomato Chutney (page 148), for serving

In a large bowl, use a large spoon to combine the yogurt, turmeric, garam masala, cumin, cayenne, salt, and lemon juice. Add the chicken and toss to coat in the yogurt mixture. Set the bowl aside and let sit for at least 15 minutes to marinate (but no more than 30 minutes or the chicken will become mushy).

In a large, heavy-bottomed saucepan or Dutch oven, heat 2 tablespoons of the butter over medium-high heat. Once the butter has melted and is bubbling, add the chicken and cook, stirring occasionally, until it begins to brown, about 4 minutes.

Use a slotted spoon or tongs to transfer the chicken to a plate. Add the remaining 2 tablespoons of butter to the saucepan and, once it is bubbling, add the onion and cook, stirring occasionally, until it has started to soften, about 1 minute. Add the ginger, garlic, paprika, and cinnamon and continue to cook for 1 minute more.

Return the chicken to the saucepan and add the tomatoes. Bring to a boil, scraping up any brown bits sticking to the pan. Cook, stirring occasionally, until the chicken is cooked through and the sauce has thickened, 8 to 10 minutes. Reduce the heat to medium-low, stir in the cream, and cook for 1 minute more, or until everything is hot.

Transfer the chicken and the sauce to plates or bowls. Top each serving with the cilantro and serve with steamed basmati rice and Sweet Tomato Chutney.

YES WAY VEGAN CHILI

You'd think it was meat if you didn't know better. This chili is made with the undeliciously named textured vegetable protein, aka soy crumbles. It's a throwback to the '70s that comes in dehydrated form, is inexpensive, takes on whatever flavors it's cooked with, and has the same texture as ground meat. Get past the sound of it and you'll love this chili, especially topped with shredded cheese and sour cream (if you don't want to keep it vegan or dairy-free) and Fritos for dipping.

SERVES 6

3 tablespoons vegetable oil

1 yellow onion, chopped

4 garlic cloves, chopped

1 tablespoon chili powder *(ancho is extra good)*

1 canned chipotle pepper in adobo, chopped

1 *(6-ounce can)* tomato paste

1 teaspoon dried oregano

1 teaspoon ground cumin

½ teaspoon ground cinnamon

1 teaspoon smoked paprika

1 tablespoon unsweetened cocoa powder

2 teaspoons kosher salt

½ teaspoon freshly ground black pepper

1 *(15-ounce)* can diced tomatoes, with their juice

1 *(15-ounce)* can pinto, black, cannellini, or kidney beans

1 cup beer

2 cups vegetable broth or water

1 bay leaf

1 tablespoon apple cider vinegar

1 to 1½ cups textured vegetable protein, such as Bob's Red Mill TVP

Shredded cheese, sour cream, and Fritos, for serving *(optional)*

In a large saucepan over medium-high heat, heat the oil until it shimmers. Add the onion and garlic and cook, stirring occasionally, until they are just beginning to brown. Add the chili powder and stir for 1 minute, until fragrant.

Add the chipotle pepper, tomato paste, oregano, cumin, cinnamon, paprika, cocoa powder, salt, black pepper, tomatoes, beans, beer, broth or water, and the bay leaf. Cover, reduce the heat to medium-low, and let simmer for about 1 hour, until the beans have softened and the flavors have married (i.e., totally blended into peak-bliss flavor happiness).

Remove the chili from the heat and discard the bay leaf. Add the vinegar and 1 cup of the textured vegetable protein. It will absorb almost immediately; add the remaining ½ cup if you like it thicker. If you don't have dietary restrictions, serve with shredded cheese, sour cream, and Fritos.

STEAMED LION'S HEAD MEATBALLS

If you like Chinese pork dumplings, you'll looooove these. If you've never used the scooping-and-slamming technique for mixing meatballs, it's what gives them that perfect, pillowy-soft texture. You'll have to cook the meatballs in two batches, unless you have a double-decker steamer. If you don't have a steamer, you can simmer them in a pot of chicken broth for 25 to 30 minutes. Add the bok choy in the last 5 minutes of cooking.

MAKES 12 MEATBALLS

1 pound ground pork (*not lean*)

2 scallions, ends trimmed, chopped

1½ teaspoons freshly grated ginger

1 large garlic clove, finely chopped

1 teaspoon kosher salt

½ teaspoon freshly ground black pepper

1 tablespoon mirin or Chinese sweet cooking wine

1½ teaspoons toasted sesame oil

2 tablespoons tamari or soy sauce

1 teaspoon packed brown sugar

1 large egg white

1 tablespoon cornstarch

4 bunches of baby bok choy, halved, or 4 sturdy leaves of savoy or napa cabbage

MAKE IT ON THE STOVE: In a large bowl, combine the pork, scallions, ginger, garlic, salt, pepper, mirin, oil, tamari, brown sugar, egg white, and cornstarch with a wooden spoon. Scoop up the mixture and slam it back down into the bowl. Repeat this technique for a full 5 minutes.

In a large saucepan with a steamer, bring 6 cups of water to a boil.

Meanwhile, using a small ice cream scoop or two soup spoons (or your hands, but make sure they're cold so the meat doesn't stick), form the pork mixture into 12 meatballs and arrange them on a plate.

Once the water has come to a boil, arrange 4 of the bok choy halves, cut side up, in the top of the steamer. Place 6 of the meatballs on top of the bok choy. Cover the steamer and let the meatballs steam for 25 to 30 minutes, or until tender and cooked through. Repeat with the remaining 4 bok choy halves and 6 meatballs.

Transfer 2 bok choy halves to a shallow bowl and pile 3 meatballs in the center. (The bok choy is the lion's mane; the meatballs are his face. See?) Repeat with the remaining meatballs and bok choy.

MAKE IT IN A RICE COOKER: If your rice cooker has a steamer basket, just follow the directions in the above recipe, using the rice cooker instead of the saucepan.

BEEF, BEER & BACON STEW

There are a few things to remember when you're making a slow-braised stew like this: a flavorful cut of meat, such as chuck, a good sear in the first step, and, to make it fork-tender, low-and-slow cooking.

SERVES 6

2 tablespoons all-purpose flour

1½ teaspoons kosher salt

Freshly ground black pepper

2 pounds beef stew meat, in 2- to 3-inch chunks

1 tablespoon vegetable oil

2 thick slices of bacon, chopped

1 large yellow onion, chopped

4 garlic cloves, chopped

2 carrots, chopped

1 can (16 ounces) dark beer, such as Guinness

3 cups beef broth (store-bought is fine)

2 bay leaves

1 teaspoon dried thyme, or a few sprigs of fresh

Freshly chopped parsley, for serving

Noodles, rice, or crusty bread, for serving

In a paper or resealable plastic bag, combine the flour, salt, and pepper. Add the beef to the bag and shake to coat. (You may have to do this in a few batches.)

In a large saucepan or Dutch oven over medium-high heat, heat the oil until it shimmers. Add as much of the beef as can fit in the saucepan in one layer (don't crowd the pan or the meat will steam rather than brown) and cook for 3 to 4 minutes on each side, flipping to cook all sides evenly, until very well browned. Transfer the browned beef to a plate and repeat with the remaining pieces, leaving the oil and the rendered beef fat in the saucepan when you transfer the browned beef to the plate.

Add the bacon to the saucepan and cook, stirring occasionally, until it has crisped up and is beginning to brown. Add the onion, garlic, and carrots, and cook, stirring occasionally, until everything is beginning to soften and brown, about 3 minutes.

Add the beer, beef broth, bay leaves, and thyme and bring to a boil, scraping up the brown bits stuck to the bottom of the pan. Let cook for about 10 minutes, then return the beef to the saucepan. Cover, reduce the heat to medium-low, and simmer until the beef is tender and the liquid has thickened, about 2 hours. Remove and discard the bay leaves.

Divide the stew among bowls and top each with the parsley. Serve with noodles or rice, or with crusty bread.

CAULIFLOWER "RICE" RISOTTO

By now you must have heard of cauliflower "rice"—cauliflower stems and florets that have been blitzed in a food processor until they resemble small grains of rice. A rice-lover like me will never mistake cauliflower for real rice, but what cauliflower does have going for it (besides the nutrients) is how well it gets along with butter, cream, and cheese. Somewhere between risotto and cauliflower mornay lives this buttery, creamy, cheesy hybrid. Don't overcook it; it's the al dente texture of the tender-crisp cauliflower that resembles that of risotto.

SERVES 2

4 tablespoons
(½ stick) salted butter

Half of a medium yellow
onion, chopped

2 cups fresh cauliflower
rice *(see Tip)*

Kosher salt and freshly
ground black pepper

½ cup chicken or
vegetable broth

½ cup heavy cream

¼ cup grated Parmesan

In a large skillet over medium-high heat, melt 3 tablespoons of the butter. Add the onion and cook, stirring occasionally, until it has turned a nice deep brown, about 5 minutes. You want to coax as much flavor as you can out of it since the cauliflower itself is bland.

TIP *To make your own cauliflower rice, cut raw cauliflower into chunks and blitz it in a food processor, or grate it on the large holes of a box grater. One medium cauliflower yields about 5 cups of rice.*

Add the cauliflower rice, season with a pinch each of salt and pepper, and stir. Cook for 1 to 2 minutes more, until the cauliflower is starting to become translucent and no longer looks raw.

Slowly add ¼ cup of the broth and cook and stir until it is almost completely absorbed, 1 to 2 minutes. Repeat with the remaining ¼ cup of broth and cook until absorbed. Add the cream and stir to incorporate. Bring the risotto to a boil and cook, stirring occasionally, for 4 to 5 minutes more, until the cream is reduced by half and the risotto has thickened.

Remove the risotto from the heat and add the remaining 1 tablespoon of butter and the Parmesan. Stir until the butter and cheese have melted. Taste the risotto and season with additional salt and pepper as desired. Serve immediately.

Variations

MUSHROOM RISOTTO: Follow the recipe, but first soak a few dried shiitake mushrooms in ⅔ cup of water for 1 hour. Drain the mushrooms, reserving the soaking liquid, and chop them before adding them to the saucepan along with the onion. Use ½ cup of the mushroom soaking liquid in place of the chicken or vegetable broth. Top the finished risotto with fresh thyme or freshly chopped parsley.

BUTTERNUT SQUASH OR PUMPKIN RISOTTO: Follow the recipe, but add ¼ cup butternut squash or canned pumpkin purée and a pinch of nutmeg when you add the cauliflower to the saucepan. Use pecorino Romano cheese in place of Parmesan.

PEA AND PESTO RISOTTO: Follow the recipe, but add a handful of frozen peas when you add the cauliflower. Add a couple of tablespoons of store-bought pesto when you stir in the cheese. Top the finished risotto with some freshly torn basil.

CHICKPEA PANCAKES

You'll need chickpea flour to make these. Known also as garbanzo bean flour, gram flour, or besan, you can find it at any Indian or Middle Eastern market and most health food stores. This stuff is packed with protein and has a nutty, earthy flavor that pairs well with dried fruits, spices, nuts, and honey as well as sautéed greens, hot chiles, and pungent herbs such as cilantro. I often make these for breakfast, topped with thick yogurt, walnuts, and date sugar; but they can of course be made savory, too.

MAKES TWO 8-INCH PANCAKES

¾ cup cold water

¼ cup plain yogurt (regular or Greek)

1 cup chickpea flour

½ teaspoon kosher salt

½ teaspoon baking soda

1 tablespoon olive or coconut oil

In a small bowl, whisk the water and yogurt until smooth. Add the chickpea flour, the salt, and the baking soda and continue to whisk until the batter is smooth. (You can make the batter up to a day ahead and keep it, covered, in the fridge.)

Heat ½ tablespoon of the oil in an 8-inch nonstick skillet over medium-high heat until it shimmers. Pour half of the batter into the skillet, tilting the pan around so the batter covers the bottom. Let cook until the edges have started to brown and are pulling away from the sides of the pan, about 3 minutes. Slip a silicone spatula under the pancake and flip it over. (It'll be easy, promise!)

Continue to cook the pancake until the underside is browned and crisped, another 2 to 3 minutes.

Transfer the finished pancake to a plate and set aside. Add the remaining ½ tablespoon of oil to the skillet and repeat the process with the remaining batter. Serve immediately or keep warm.

Variations

SPICED CARROT AND GOLDEN RAISIN PANCAKE: Add 1 teaspoon of garam masala, 1 grated carrot, and 1 tablespoon of golden raisins to the batter. Serve the finished pancakes with additional plain yogurt and Sweet Tomato Chutney (page 148).

JALAPEÑO, CILANTRO, AND GINGER PANCAKE: Add 1 teaspoon of freshly grated ginger, 1 teaspoon of chopped fresh jalapeño (seeded), and a small handful of chopped cilantro to the batter. Serve the finished pancakes with additional plain yogurt and Pickled Tink Onions (page 150), or any fruit pickles such as mango or lime.

CURRY, SMASHED POTATO, AND GREENS PANCAKE: Increase the oil to 2 tablespoons. First, heat 1 tablespoon of the oil over medium-high heat. Add leftover baked potatoes (skin on, smashed with your hands) and add ½ teaspoon curry powder and season with salt and pepper. Cook until the potatoes start to brown and crisp. Add a handful of torn Swiss chard or spinach and cook for 1 minute more. Transfer half of this mixture to a plate, then pour half of the batter into the pan and proceed as in the main recipe. Repeat with the remaining batter and the remaining potato mixture.

SOLO & PORTABLE MEALS

RICE PAPER SALAD ROLLS

These rolls are a little tricky, or at least a small project, but so worth mastering. The rice paper wrappers are hard disks that look like translucent plastic tortillas. You'll find them in Asian markets and in the Asian section of most major supermarkets. The tricky bit is softening them: You dunk them quickly in hot water and lay them on a damp, lint-free kitchen towel to fill and roll. Dunking too long makes them dissolve; too little and they're too brittle to roll. If you find they're too brittle, spray them with a bit of water from a spray bottle. Practice until you get the hang of it—and be patient. You can add thin strips of cooked chicken, seafood, meat, or baked tofu to the rolls, too. Serve with Bang Bang Sauce for dipping.

MAKES 4 ROLLS

1 ounce rice vermicelli noodles, cellophane noodles, or bean threads

8 *(8-inch)* rice paper wrappers *(use 4 to practice, and 4 to serve)*

4 leaves of romaine, butter, Little Gem, or Boston lettuce

Half of a small cucumber, peeled, seeded, and cut into thin strips

Half of a mango, peeled and cut into thin strips

Half of an avocado, peeled and cut into 8 thin wedges

Fresh mint, basil, and/or cilantro leaves (any combination)

Bang Bang Sauce *(page 144)*, for serving

Put the vermicelli noodles into a large heatproof bowl or pie plate. Pour enough boiling hot water over the noodles to cover them. Let the noodles soak while you get all your ingredients prepped and ready to roll (pun intended).

Wet a clean dish towel, wring it out, and lay it flat on a work surface. After about 10 minutes of soaking, lift the vermicelli out of the bowl, reserving the water, and place in a separate bowl.

Now for the fun: Dip one of the rice paper wrappers *for just a second or two* in the bowl with the warm water and place it on the damp towel. It will continue to soften on the towel. Arrange a leaf of lettuce and a quarter each of the vermicelli, cucumber, mango, avocado, and herbs in a row across the center of the rice paper wrapper, leaving a couple of inches on the sides uncovered. Fold those sides toward the center over the filling, then tightly roll the wrapper, from the bottom up, like a burrito.

Set the roll aside on a plate lined with a dampened paper towel while you make the rest of the rolls.

Repeat these steps with the other 3 wrappers and the remaining ingredients. Serve with Bang Bang Sauce.

TIP *Make this GF by using GF bread.*

WAFFLE-IRON
GRILLED CHEESE SANDWICH

The thing about using a waffle iron here is that by some miracle of physics it turns out a grilled cheese that has even more crispy, buttery surface area than you get with a flat skillet. You'll easily want another one of these in the same sitting, so feel free to double the recipe and just make one sandwich in the waffle iron at a time. You could also make this in an electric skillet (four at a time!) or the old-school way: Wrap your sandwich in nonstick foil and hit it for about two minutes on each side with a clothing iron, set on the highest heat level, without steam. Crazy but true!

MAKES 1 SANDWICH

1 tablespoon salted butter, at room temperature

2 slices good-quality white or wheat bread *(or potato bread, if you can find it)*

2 ounces good-quality melting cheese, such as Cheddar, fontina, Jack, Havarti, or mozzarella

Dijon mustard or Sweet Tomato Chutney *(page 148)*, **for serving**

Preheat the waffle iron while you assemble the sandwich.

Butter one side of each piece of bread and put the cheese in the middle, with the buttered sides of the bread facing out.

Place the sandwich in the center of the waffle iron, pressing down a bit as it cooks, and cook for about 2 minutes, until the bread is toasted and golden brown and the cheese has melted (it's okay to peek). Transfer the grilled cheese to a plate and serve with Dijon mustard or Sweet Tomato Chutney.

Variations

GOUDA AND APPLE: Spread some honey mustard on the unbuttered sides of the bread and add a couple of very thin slices of tart apple, such as Granny Smith, along with 2 ounces of sliced Gouda. Proceed as above.

HAM, GRUYÈRE, AND CRISPY ONIONS: Spread Dijon mustard on the unbuttered sides of the bread. Arrange a thin slice of ham, a slice of Gruyère, and a sprinkling of store-bought crispy fried onions on top of the mustard, then add a second layer of Gruyère and ham. (The onions stay crispy this way.) Proceed as above.

SALAMI, PROVOLONE, AND PEPPERS: Instead of butter, brush the bread with extra-virgin olive oil. Put a slice or two of salami (Genoa, pepperoni, or soppressata), provolone, and a couple of chopped pickled hot peppers (such as peperoncini or cherry peppers) in the middle and proceed as above.

ROASTED CAULIFLOWER,

LOTS OF WAYS

Lots of cooks have taken to roasting whole heads of cauliflower, but I prefer the look of quarters. Besides, smaller pieces cook faster, and there's more surface area to get nice and roasty.

SERVES 2

1 head of cauliflower

3 tablespoons extra-virgin olive oil

1 teaspoon kosher salt

Freshly ground black pepper

Preheat the oven to 375°F and line a sheet pan with nonstick foil. Trim off the stem of the cauliflower as well as the large, thick leaves (the tender, smaller ones are fine to keep on), then cut the cauliflower in quarters, top to bottom.

Rub the oil, salt, and pepper up and down and all around the cauliflower segments. Arrange the cauliflower, cut sides down, on the sheet pan. Roast until the cauliflower is nice and brown, crispy on the edges and soft in the middle (pierce it at the thickest part of the stem with a knife; it should offer no resistance), 35 to 40 minutes. Transfer to a plate and serve.

Variations

GARLICKY PARM: In a small bowl, combine ¼ cup mayonnaise, 1 teaspoon garlic powder, 1 teaspoon paprika (smoked is really good here), ¼ cup grated Parmesan, and ½ teaspoon kosher salt and stir until smooth. Slather this up and down and all around the cauliflower and proceed as above.

HOT AND SWEET MISO: In a small bowl, combine 2 tablespoons toasted sesame oil, 2 tablespoons red miso, 2 teaspoons chili-garlic paste, 1 tablespoon brown sugar, and 1 tablespoon hot water. Slather this up and down and all around the cauliflower and proceed as above. Halfway through cooking, spoon up any topping that's dripped down and dribble it back over the cauliflower.

TACO-SPICED: You'll need a packet of taco seasoning mix. Combine 2 to 3 tablespoons of the taco mix with 3 tablespoons olive oil, and slather this up and down and all around the cauliflower. Proceed as above.

HONORS RAMEN

If you're a college student, chances are you've eaten your share of ramen. Authentic ramen is based on rich, complex, slow-cooked broths and hand-pulled wheat noodles, and no sane college student is ever going to make it from scratch. Lucky for all of us, instant ramen was invented in 1958 and it's one of the cheapest meals around, even if it's full of fat and carbs and sodium. If you're going to eat it, and you probably are, at least fancy it up a bit. Here are a few ways to do just that.

EACH VARIATION SERVES 1

KIMCHI, BACON, AND EGG RAMEN

2 slices of bacon

1 Teakettle Egg *(page 151)* or 1 fried egg *(optional)*

1 package Top Ramen, chicken or beef flavor

½ cup chopped kimchi

1 teaspoon chili-garlic paste

Toasted sesame oil, for serving

In a large skillet over medium heat, fry the bacon until browned and crisp and transfer to a plate. Drain most of the fat from the skillet, and if you want a fried egg, now's the time to make it in the skillet. Transfer the finished egg to the plate with the bacon.

Add 2 cups of water, half of the Top Ramen seasoning packet, the kimchi, and the chili paste to the skillet and bring to a boil. Add the Top Ramen noodles and cook, stirring them in the broth, until soft, about 5 minutes.

Return the bacon and egg back to the pan for 1 minute just to heat up. Transfer the ramen to a bowl and drizzle with a bit of sesame oil.

(recipe continues)

STRACCIATELLA (SAY STRAH-CHA-TELLA)

1 package Top Ramen, chicken flavor

Handful of frozen peas

2 large eggs

3 tablespoons grated Parmesan or pecorino Romano cheese

Pinch of red pepper flakes (wash your hands after!), for serving

Lemon wedge, for serving

MAKE IT ON THE STOVE: In a small saucepan over medium heat, bring 2 cups of water and the contents of the Top Ramen seasoning packet to a boil. Add the handful of frozen peas and the Top Ramen noodles and cook, stirring the noodles in the broth until soft, about 5 minutes.

Meanwhile, in a coffee mug, use a fork to whisk the eggs and cheese together. When the noodles are done, keep the water at a slow boil while you perform the following trick: With one hand, pour the egg mixture into the soup in a steady stream while using your other hand to stir the soup around gently with the fork. The eggs will form little "rags" and cook almost immediately. Transfer the ramen to a bowl and sprinkle with the red pepper flakes and a squeeze of the lemon wedge.

MAKE IT IN A RICE COOKER: Set your rice cooker to Cook mode and add 2 cups of water and the contents of the Top Ramen seasoning packet.

When it comes to a boil, stir in the peas and Top Ramen noodles and proceed as in the above recipe. It will take a few seconds longer to cook the eggs (and the "rags" will be tattered instead of shredded—tastes the same though!).

RED CURRY COCONUT

1 teaspoon red curry paste

1 package Top Ramen, shrimp flavor

Handful of green beans, trimmed

5 raw, peeled shrimp (optional; if the budget can swing it)

¼ cup canned coconut milk

Lime wedge, for serving

Fresh mint and basil leaves, for serving

Peanuts, for serving (optional)

MAKE IT ON THE STOVE: In a small saucepan over medium heat, bring 2 cups of water, the curry paste, and half of the Top Ramen seasoning packet to a boil. Add the handful of green beans and cook for 1 to 2 minutes, until tender. Add the Top Ramen noodles and cook, stirring them in the broth until soft, about 5 minutes.

Add the shrimp, if using, and when they curl up and become opaque, stir in the coconut milk. Transfer the ramen to a bowl and top with a good squeeze of lime, the herbs, and the peanuts if you like.

MAKE IT IN A RICE COOKER: Set your rice cooker to Cook mode. Bring 2 cups of water, the curry paste, and half of the Top Ramen seasoning packet to a boil, then proceed as instructed above. It will take your shrimp a minute more to cook but #NoBiggie!

CAPRESE GARLIC BREAD

Is it weird to eat salad on bread? I don't think so. Croutons are bread *with* salad, right? Here's something that's a cross between a sandwich, a salad, and a slice of pizza—but better. You've got hot, buttery, garlicky toast with cool tomatoes, basil, and mozzarella that just begins to melt when it hits the bread. You'll need a knife and fork for this one!

SERVES 1

1 tablespoon unsalted butter, at room temperature

1 teaspoon garlic powder, or 1 finely chopped garlic clove

Kosher salt

A nice thick slice of crusty bread

3 slices of the best tomato you can find

3 slices of fresh mozzarella *(water-packed is best)*

Freshly torn basil leaves

Extra-virgin olive oil

Freshly ground black pepper

MAKE IT ON THE STOVE: In a small bowl, combine the butter, garlic, and salt and use a fork to incorporate everything into the butter.

Heat a medium skillet over medium heat and spread both sides of the bread with the garlic butter. Toast the bread in the skillet for 2 minutes on each side, or until both sides are as browned and crisp as you like.

Remove the skillet from the heat and transfer the bread to a plate. Arrange the tomato and mozzarella in alternate layers on top of the bread. Top with the basil and a drizzle of olive oil, and sprinkle with additional salt and a few good turns of the pepper mill.

MAKE IT IN A WAFFLE IRON: Follow the directions in the above recipe, except instead of toasting the bread in a skillet, toast it in a preheated waffle iron for 2 to 3 minutes. Remember to give the waffle iron a good cleaning afterward, to get rid of the garlic.

TIP *Make this GF by using GF bread.*

FALAFEL BURGERS

So one day I'm thinking how brilliant it would be to make a veggie burger out of chickpeas, when I remembered that such a thing already exists: falafel! *#duh*. This recipe IS brilliant, if I do say so myself; hummus already has the chickpeas and most of the flavors of falafel, and the crushed cornflakes give you that crunchy texture. Don't be afraid to experiment with any flavored hummus, if you'd like to mix it up from plain.

SERVES 5

2 cups cornflakes

1 *(10-ounce)* **container of hummus**

1 large egg

3 tablespoons finely chopped cilantro

1 teaspoon ground coriander

Vegetable oil, for frying

FOR SERVING

Burger bun, pita, or flour tortilla *(optional)*

Pickled Tink Onions *(page 150)*

Falafel Cart White Sauce *(recipe follows)*

Harissa or other hot sauce *(optional)*

Lettuce and tomato slices

Pour the cornflakes into a sealable zipper bag and close the seal. Crunch the bag in your hands until the cornflakes are the size of bread crumbs. (A few larger pieces are fine.) Place 1 cup of the crushed cornflakes in a shallow bowl and set aside.

In a large bowl, combine the hummus, egg, cilantro, coriander, and the remaining 1 cup of cornflakes. Form the mixture into 5 patties, about 3 inches in diameter and ½ inch thick. Coat 1 patty at a time in the crushed cornflakes, pressing them into the patties on all sides. Arrange the patties on a plate or sheet pan and refrigerate for up to 6 hours, tightly covered, or cook immediately.

In a large skillet, heat ½ inch of vegetable oil over medium heat until the oil is shimmering. Add the falafel patties, being careful not to crowd the pan (you may have to do this in two batches), and let them sizzle away for about 2 minutes on each side, until nicely browned and crunchy. Use tongs to transfer them to a paper towel–lined plate while you cook the rest.

Serve each falafel patty in a bun along with Pickled Tink Onions, Falafel Cart White Sauce, harissa, lettuce, and/or tomato, as desired.

Falafel Cart White Sauce
MAKES ½ CUP

¼ cup mayonnaise

¼ cup plain Greek
yogurt

1 teaspoon sugar

1 tablespoon distilled
white vinegar

1 teaspoon kosher salt

Freshly ground
black pepper

Whisk the mayonnaise, yogurt, sugar, vinegar, salt, and pepper until combined. Store, covered, in the fridge for up to 2 weeks.

MISO SOUP

If you've ever been to a sushi bar, you've had miso soup—that savory, slightly smoky broth with cubes of tofu and seaweed. Miso soup has tons of nutrients and is a great afternoon snack or even breakfast on a chilly day. Traditionally, it's made with miso paste and dashi, a broth made of dried fish and seaweed. Do it the easy way by starting with Hondashi, dashi granules. Make sure you don't boil the soup after adding the miso or it will separate.

MAKES 2 CUPS

1 teaspoon
Hondashi granules

2 tablespoons
miso paste

OPTIONAL ADD-INS

Wakame *(dried seaweed)*, soaked in warm water for 5 minutes and drained; diced tofu; dried shiitake mushrooms, soaked in warm water for 15 minutes and sliced; cooked carrots, potato, sweet potato, parsnip, broccoli, or spinach; a Teakettle Egg *(page 000)*; scallions; crispy onions; sesame seeds; lotus root; or whatever else you fancy.

In a small saucepan over medium heat, combine the Hondashi granules and 2 cups of water and bring to a boil. Once the water is boiling, remove from the heat and immediately add the miso and whisk until combined.

MAKE IT IN A RICE COOKER: Set the rice cooker to the Cook mode and add 2 cups of water and the Hondashi granules. It will take 4 to 5 minutes to come up to a boil, and when it does, turn the rice cooker off and then whisk in the miso.

MAKE IT WITH A TEAKETTLE: Put the Hondashi granules in the bowl you'll use to eat the miso. Boil 2 cups of water in your teakettle and stir it into the Hondashi. Immediately whisk in the miso.

WHO NEEDS RED BULL?

BRAIN FOOD FOR DAYTIME OR LATE-NIGHT SNACKING

VIM BALLS

So much better than cookies or candy, these sweet little nuggets of energy give you Vim and Vigor and good things like antioxidants and iron to keep you going. Put them in paper mini-muffin cups in a nice little box and they make a deliciously thoughtful gift.

MAKES 16

½ cup raw almonds

1¼ cups cornflakes

1½ cups medjool dates, pitted

Unsweetened cocoa powder, grated unsweetened coconut, and/or ground nuts, for rolling

In a food processor, combine the almonds and cornflakes and blitz until they're the texture of wet sand. Add the dates and blitz again until the mixture resembles a thick paste. Scrape the mixture into a bowl.

With wet hands, roll spoonfuls of the mixture into balls the size of walnuts and place on a large plate. Place the cocoa powder, grated coconut, or ground nuts (or a mix) on a plate and roll each ball around the plate to coat. Store the balls in an airtight container at room temperature for 2 weeks or in the fridge for 1 month.

TIP *Food processors come in mini sizes that are perfect for small spaces.*

Variations

TURKISH DELIGHT: Substitute ½ cup dried apricots for ½ cup of the dates, and soak the apricots in boiling water for 10 minutes and drain. Process all of the ingredients as directed, adding ½ teaspoon ground cardamom and 2 teaspoons of rose water to the mixture when adding the apricots. Roll the balls in ground pistachios.

DAYDREAMSICLE: Add the grated zest of 1 orange, 1 tablespoon unsweetened cocoa powder, and ½ teaspoon ground cinnamon to the mixture in the first step. Use more cocoa powder for rolling.

PECAN PIE: Use toasted pecans instead of almonds in the first step, and add 1 teaspoon of vanilla extract and a pinch of kosher salt when you add the dates. Use ground pecans (toasted or untoasted) for rolling.

SAVORY SEED & OAT

GRANOLA

Think of this as a sort of Superbad (meaning Good) Snack Mix, but instead of square cereal and pretzels, it's made of oats, seeds, miso, maple, and other salty, savory, sweet, and spicy things you and your body crave. I like it instead of croutons on salads and soups, and in a savory parfait with chopped tomatoes, cucumbers, and Greek yogurt.

MAKES 2½ CUPS

Nonstick cooking spray

1 cup regular rolled oats *(not quick-cooking)*

¼ cup chickpea flour

2 tablespoons chia or hemp seeds, or a mixture of both

2 tablespoons sesame seeds

½ cup pepitas or sunflower seeds, or a mixture of both

1 tablespoon fennel seeds

1 tablespoon coriander seeds

1 tablespoon cumin seeds

¼ teaspoon cayenne

2 tablespoons maple syrup or agave

1 tablespoon miso *(any type)*

2 tablespoons vegetable oil or coconut oil

1 large egg white

Preheat the oven or toaster oven to 325°F. Spray an ⅛-size sheet pan with nonstick cooking spray or line it with baking parchment.

In a large bowl, combine the oats, chickpea flour, chia seeds, sesame seeds, pepitas, fennel seeds, coriander seeds, cumin seeds, and cayenne.

In a separate bowl, whisk the maple syrup, miso, oil, 1 tablespoon of water, and the egg white. Pour this mixture into the bowl with the oats and use a silicone spatula to combine, until all of the dry ingredients are evenly coated.

Spread the granola onto the sheet pan and bake, stirring once halfway through, for 45 minutes to 1 hour, or until the granola is evenly browned and fragrant. Cool completely before transferring to a jar with a tight-fitting lid. Keeps for 2 weeks at room temperature.

TIP *Make this GF by using gluten-free miso and gluten-free oats.*

GINGERBREAD CRUSH BARS

I'm addicted to those bars that are made of fruit and nuts and energy, but they're so pricey. Who can afford that type of obsession? So I set out to create a copycat version and I'm pretty sure you couldn't tell the difference between these and the pricey ones. They taste like gingerbread, carrot cake, cherry pie, and brownies—and I'm not promising anything, but try them and I'll bet you anything you crush those midterms.

MAKES SIX 2 × 4-INCH BARS

½ cup raw almonds

½ cup raw walnuts or pecans

1 teaspoon vanilla extract

1 teaspoon ground ginger

½ teaspoon ground cinnamon

¼ teaspoon ground allspice or cloves

1 cup pitted medjool dates, packed

Pinch of kosher salt

Line an 8 × 6-inch baking dish with baking parchment so that it extends over the sides of the dish.

In a food processor, blitz the nuts until very finely ground. Add the vanilla, ginger, cinnamon, allspice, dates, and salt and blitz until it forms a ball. Scrape into the prepared baking dish and, with wet hands, press down and flatten the dough. Use the parchment hanging down the sides to cover the dough and let rest for 1 hour.

Uncover the dough and transfer it to a cutting board. Using a sharp, dampened knife, cut the dough into bars or squares and they're ready to eat! These can be stored in an airtight container for up to 2 weeks at room temperature or for a month in the fridge.

Variations

CARROT CAKE: Follow the directions, but use ½ cup almonds, ½ cup walnuts, ½ cup grated carrots (squeezed dry in a clean dish towel), 1½ teaspoons ground cinnamon, ½ cup dried pineapple (soaked for 10 minutes in boiling water and drained), ½ cup pitted medjool dates, and a pinch of kosher salt.

CHERRY PIE: Follow the directions, but use ½ cup almonds, ½ cup walnuts, ½ teaspoon ground cinnamon, 1 teaspoon vanilla extract, ½ cup dried tart cherries, ½ cup pitted medjool dates, and a pinch of kosher salt.

BROWNIES: Follow the directions, but use ½ cup almonds, ½ cup walnuts, 3 tablespoons unsweetened cocoa powder, 1½ teaspoons vanilla extract, 1¼ cups pitted medjool dates, and a pinch of kosher salt.

TIP *Food processors come in mini sizes that are perfect for small spaces.*

CHEESE CRISPS

I don't know about you, but my favorite part of lasagne is the cheese that melts onto the pan and gets browned and crispy. Same goes for grilled cheese and pizza. So why not bypass the main dish and just make those crispy bits of cheese? Asked and answered. If you can tolerate delayed gratification, make them in the toaster oven or rice cooker. If not, use the microwave. But practice delayed gratification too.

MAKES 4 CRISPS

**1 cup grated Cheddar
or Parmesan cheese**

MAKE IT IN A MICROWAVE: Line a microwave-safe plate with a silicone pan liner or baking parchment. Spread ¼ cup of the cheese evenly onto the plate to make a disk about 4 inches in diameter. Microwave for about 1 minute, until the cheese is melted and golden brown.

Let it cool for a few seconds before peeling it off the parchment. Set aside and repeat with the remaining cheese, ¼ cup at a time.

MAKE IT IN A RICE COOKER: Parmesan works better than Cheddar for this method. Set the rice cooker to Cook mode and spread ¼ cup of the cheese evenly in the pot. Cover and let cook until the cheese is bubbling and has turned golden brown, 4 to 5 minutes.

Remove the pot from the rice cooker and let the cheese cool until it has crisped up and can be lifted out of the pot with a fork, 3 to 4 minutes. Repeat with the remaining cheese, ¼ cup at a time. (Since the cooker is now hot, the 3 remaining batches of cheese will crisp up in 3 to 4 minutes.)

Variations

PEPPER PARM: Use Parmesan instead of Cheddar and season with a few turns of the pepper mill. Microwave for 45 seconds.

TACO CHEESE: Use a grated Mexican cheese blend and top with a sprinkling of dry taco seasoning mix. Microwave for 1 minute or a few seconds more.

POWER-UP SHAKES

What's the difference between a smoothie and a shake? Smoothies are typically made with lots of fruit and a little milk or yogurt—not always the dairy kind—while shakes are mostly dairy, with ice cream and milk as the base. However, the word smoothie is a little silly to my ears, the way soup would if it were called soupie. While the lines are pretty much drawn, to my knowledge there are no smoothie police enforcing smoothie laws, so I'm calling these shakes.

MAKES ABOUT 2 CUPS

1 cup frozen fruit, such as sliced bananas or berries

1 cup cold coconut milk, almond milk, or kefir

1 scoop protein powder or collagen, such as Trader Joe's vanilla pea protein powder

1 to 2 teaspoons agave or maple syrup *(or date sugar, if you like it sweeter)*

Handful of greens, such as spinach or kale *(optional)*

Combine the fruit, coconut milk, protein powder, agave, and greens (if using) in a blender and blitz until smooth.

Turn off the blender and scrape down any large bits with a silicone spatula, then blitz for a few seconds longer. Transfer to a glass or glasses and serve.

Variations

MATCHA LATTE SHAKE: Follow the directions, but use ¾ cup of frozen banana slices (from 1 large banana), a small handful of spinach leaves, 2 teaspoons Chinese green tea powder (I like this better than ceremonial grade—aka expensive—Japanese matcha. Tastes like green tea ice cream!), 1 scoop protein powder, 1 teaspoon agave, and 1 cup coconut milk.

DROP THE BEET SHAKE: Follow the directions, but use 1 cup frozen raspberries or strawberries, 1 teaspoon beet powder, 1 scoop protein powder, and 1 cup coconut milk.

GOLDEN TEMPLE SHAKE: Follow the directions, but use 1 cup frozen banana slices, 2 teaspoons date sugar or 1 pitted date, 1 teaspoon ground turmeric, ¼ teaspoon ground cardamom, and 1 cup coconut or almond milk. Season with freshly ground pepper.

#REBOOTEA

This is just the thing when you're feeling poorly. Take it by the tablespoonful as a healing tonic, or add to boiling water as a cleansing tea. It's also good over ice with a splash of fizzy water. Ginger has anti-nausea and anti-inflammatory properties, lemon helps cut through a cough and has loads of vitamin C to help you recover and reboot, and besides soothing your throat, honey and cayenne are antibacterial. The combination of lemon, ginger, and honey is also said to boost your immune system. Most of all, it tastes good. Would I recommend anything that didn't?

MAKES 2 CUPS

1 *(4-inch)* **piece of ginger, cut crosswise into coins**

½ cup honey

Juice of 1 lemon

¼ teaspoon cayenne

In a large saucepan over medium heat, combine 3 cups of water with the ginger and honey. Stir and bring to a boil.

Reduce the heat to medium-low and let the tea bubble away for 20 minutes, or until reduced by about a third. Add the lemon juice and cayenne and continue to simmer for 5 minutes more.

Remove the saucepan from the heat, and remove and discard the ginger. Pour the tea into mugs to enjoy now, or into an airtight container to keep in the fridge for up to 1 month.

LASSI

At first glance a lassi may seem just like a smoothie or a shake, but it's a category all its own. Lassis are always made with yogurt and they are meant to be on the tart side. They never ever contain protein powder or ground flaxseeds or anything that would share a sentence with the word "wellness," but they're about as naturally healthful as you can get. The other thing that sets them apart from shakes and smoothies is that they are often savory instead of sweet, in which case they are typically called chaas. There's nothing more refreshing on a sticky summer day than chaas.

MAKES ABOUT 2½ CUPS

1 cup plain whole-milk yogurt (*not Greek or strained yogurt*)

½ cup milk or buttermilk

1 cup ice cubes or frozen fruit

Sugar, agave, maple syrup, or date sugar, to taste

Kosher salt

A squeeze of lemon or lime, if you like it tart

Combine the yogurt, milk, ice, sugar (start with a tablespoon or so; you can add more later), a pinch of salt, and the lemon juice (if using) in a blender and blitz it until it's smooth.

Turn off the blender and scrape down any large bits with a silicone spatula, then blitz for a few seconds longer. Taste for sweetness and add more sugar or sweetener as desired, stirring to incorporate. Transfer to glasses to serve.

Variations

MANGO LASSI: Follow the directions, but use frozen mangoes instead of ice, milk instead of buttermilk, 1 tablespoon sugar or another sweetener (or more if you like it sweeter), and add ¼ teaspoon ground cardamom.

STRAWBERRY ROSE LASSI: Follow the directions, but use frozen strawberries instead of ice, milk instead of buttermilk, 1 tablespoon sugar or another sweetener, and add ½ teaspoon rose water.

CHAAS: Follow the directions, but use ice cubes and buttermilk and a pinch of salt, and add a dash of cayenne, a few mint leaves, and a good squeeze of lemon.

HACK-UCCINO

 GF **VG**

To get the same über-smooth consistency as the coffee bars do, you really need to make this in a high-speed blender or bullet. That shouldn't discourage you, though; you can get pretty close with a conventional one. If you've never used sweetened condensed milk, try it here. It gives the drink a smoother texture and a faint caramel-like flavor. And please get in the habit of using a reusable straw!

MAKES ENOUGH FOR 1 TO 2 PEOPLE & SAVES YOU ABOUT $4

1 cup cold milk, any kind

1 tablespoon instant espresso powder dissolved in 1 cup water, or ½ cup liquid cold brew concentrate mixed with ½ cup water

2 to 3 tablespoons sweetened condensed milk, maple syrup, or agave

2 cups ice

Whipped cream, for serving

Combine the milk, espresso, condensed milk, and ice in a blender and blitz until the ice is broken up and the mixture is thick.

Turn off the blender and scrape down any unblended bits with a silicone spatula, then blitz for a few seconds longer until completely smooth. Transfer to glasses and serve with whipped cream on top.

Variations

MOCHA HACK-UCCINO: Follow the directions, but add 2 tablespoons of the Chocolate Ganache (page 142) and use 2 tablespoons of the sweetener of your choice. When done blending, transfer to glasses and garnish with cocoa powder or crushed chocolate-covered espresso beans.

PEPPERMINT MOCHA HACK-UCCINO: Follow the directions, but add 2 tablespoons of Chocolate Ganache (page 142) and a few drops of peppermint extract. Use 2 tablespoons of the sweetener of your choice. When done blending, transfer to glasses and garnish with a peppermint stick or crushed peppermint candy.

CARAMEL HACK-UCCINO: Follow the directions, but use 4 tablespoons of the Dulce de Leche (page 133) in place of other sweeteners. When done blending, transfer to glasses and garnish with crushed peanut brittle.

#PSL: Follow the directions, but add ⅓ cup canned pumpkin purée, 1 teaspoon pumpkin pie spice, and 1 teaspoon vanilla. Use condensed milk for the sweetener.

TIP *If the chickpeas lose their crunch a bit as leftovers, just toast them on a sheet pan in a 375°F oven for 10 minutes to re-crisp.*

ROASTED CHICKPEAS

Here's a good alternative to roasted nuts if allergy or preference keeps you away. Roasting chickpeas brings out their nuttiness, and even when roasted, their creaminess comes through. If you're using a regular-size oven, feel free to double the recipe and use a bigger sheet pan.

MAKES 1½ CUPS

½ cup dried chickpeas

1 tablespoon extra-virgin olive oil

½ teaspoon kosher salt

Freshly ground black pepper

Rinse the chickpeas and soak in cold water at room temperature overnight (or for 10 hours). The next day, preheat the oven or toaster oven to 375°F.

Drain the chickpeas and pat them dry. In a medium bowl, combine the chickpeas, olive oil, salt, and a few good turns of the pepper mill and stir to coat.

Spread the chickpeas out on an ⅛-size sheet pan. Roast for about 45 minutes, stirring the chickpeas once halfway through, until they are browned and crispy.

Serve immediately, or let cool completely before storing, tightly covered, at room temperature for up to 1 week.

Variations

MASALA CHICKPEAS: Follow the directions above, but add 1 teaspoon garam masala, ½ teaspoon ground cumin, and ¼ teaspoon cayenne along with the salt and pepper.

SWEET AND SMOKY CHICKPEAS: Follow the directions above, but add 2 teaspoons smoked paprika, ½ teaspoon garlic powder, and 2 tablespoons sugar along with the salt and pepper. Stir every 10 minutes to prevent the sugar from burning.

HOT CURRY CHICKPEAS: Follow the directions above, but add 2 teaspoons curry powder and ½ teaspoon cayenne along with the salt and pepper.

NOTE *You need to plan a day ahead to make these. #sorrynotsorry. You won't be boiling them; they go from soaking to roasting, so they need a good 10 hours to soak. Don't be tempted to use canned chickpeas for this. They contain too much moisture to really get crunchy when you roast them—and they stay that way.*

PAPER BAG POPCORN

I confess I own a microwave for these two purposes: to melt butter and chocolate for baking, and to make popcorn. If you've been buying microwave popcorn, stop. right.now! It contains all sorts of things you don't need to put in your body and it's pricey. Really pricey. Better to pop your own and top it with melted butter, or one of the three flavored butters below. All it takes is a paper lunch bag and two tablespoons of popping corn. You can—and please do—use the same bag over and over.

MAKES ABOUT 5 CUPS

2 tablespoons popping corn

Kosher salt

2 tablespoons unsalted butter, melted

Pour the popcorn into a paper lunch bag and roll the top down a few inches to close tightly.

Microwave on High or on the popcorn setting for 2 to 2½ minutes, or until the popping sounds are few and far between and have nearly stopped.

Sprinkle the popcorn with salt and transfer to a bowl. Pour in the butter and stir to coat.

Variations

BADA BING BANG POPCORN: Before you pop the popcorn, melt 2 tablespoons unsalted butter with ½ teaspoon garlic powder and ½ teaspoon kosher salt in the microwave. Pour into the bowl with the popped corn, along with some grated Parmesan and red pepper flakes, and toss to coat.

MAPLE MISO POPCORN: Before you pop the popcorn, combine 2 tablespoons of unsalted butter with 2 tablespoons maple syrup and 1 teaspoon miso in a small bowl. Microwave the butter until melted, about 15 seconds. Stir once more before pouring into the bowl with the popped corn. Season with smoked salt if you like.

HOT CURRY POPCORN: Before you pop the popcorn, melt 2 tablespoons unsalted butter with 1 teaspoon curry powder and ¼ teaspoon cayenne in the microwave. Pour into the bowl with the popped corn and toss to coat. Sprinkle with black lava salt because *#yellowandblacklookcool*.

SWEET THINGS

BANANA NUTELLA CHILL CAKE

VG

I do love a bit of culinary trickery. Like when you bake a cake with cookies and it's not baked? This, young grasshopper, is such a thing. When it was invented in the 1930s, refrigerators (then called iceboxes) were chilled with big blocks of ice, and fridge manufacturers developed this sort of dessert to entice homemakers and encourage sales. At its simplest, the classic icebox cake is made with sweetened whipped cream and cookies, which soften in the cream and take on a cake-like texture in the fridge. I love the combination of bananas and Nutella, and that's what inspired the cake here. The first variation features the magical combo of chocolate, coffee, and dulce de leche, and the other is a riff on a strawberry shortcake. Once the cake is assembled, both you and the cake can just sit back and chill.

SERVES 6

2 cups heavy cream

1¼ cups Nutella

½ cup coffee

1 (14.3-ounce) package Oreo cookies

2 bananas, sliced

Handful of banana chips, crushed, or chopped toasted almonds, for serving

Line an 8 × 4-inch loaf pan with baking parchment, with an overhang on the sides for wrapping.

In a large bowl, with an electric handheld mixer or a whisk (it'll take some elbow grease, but it'll work!), whip the cream and 1 cup of the Nutella until the mixture is stiff.

Pour the coffee into a small, shallow bowl. Briefly dip the Oreos, one by one, into the coffee and set aside on a cutting board.

Line the bottom of the pan with a third of the Nutella cream mixture. Make a second layer with a third of the Oreos, trimming them to fit snugly. (Cut some of them in half so the cut sides butt up against the perimeter of the pan.) Top the layer of cookies with half of the sliced bananas.

Repeat to form another layer with the remaining Nutella cream mixture, another third of the Oreos, and the remaining sliced bananas. Top with the remaining Oreos.

(recipe continues)

Fold the overhanging baking parchment over the cake, tuck it into the sides to cover, and refrigerate overnight or up to 2 days.

When ready to serve, unwrap the cake and turn it out onto a serving plate. Stir the remaining ¼ cup Nutella vigorously to loosen it up, pour it on the cake, and decorate the top with the banana chips or almonds.

Variations

DIRTY DULCE CHILL CAKE

½ cup cold-brewed coffee	1 teaspoon vanilla extract
½ cup plus 2 tablespoons Dulce de Leche (*page 133*), plus more for serving	1 (*14.3-ounce*) package Oreo cookies
2 cups heavy cream	Chocolate-covered espresso beans, for serving

Line an 8 × 4-inch loaf pan with baking parchment, with an overhang on the sides for wrapping. Pour the coffee into a shallow bowl.

In a large bowl, with an electric handheld mixer or a whisk, combine the dulce de leche, cream, and vanilla and whip until the mixture is combined and stiff. Line the bottom of the pan with a third of the whipped cream. Dip a third of the cookies quickly on both sides in the coffee, then place them snugly in a layer on top of the cream. (Cut some of them in half so the cut sides butt up against the perimeter of the pan.)

Make two more layers with the remaining cream and cookies. Fold the overhanging baking parchment over the cake to cover, and refrigerate overnight or up to 2 days.

When ready to serve, unwrap the cake and turn it out onto a serving plate. Stir the dulce de leche vigorously to loosen it up. Decorate the cake with a drizzle of dulce de leche and the chocolate-covered espresso beans.

STRAWBERRIES AND CREAM CHILL CAKE

½ cup milk, any kind	1 quart strawberries, tops removed, sliced, plus a few for serving
2 cups heavy cream	
½ cup powdered sugar	1 (*14.3-ounce*) package Golden Oreo cookies or classic Oreo cookies
1 teaspoon vanilla extract	

Line an 8 × 4-inch loaf pan with baking parchment, with an overhang on the sides for wrapping. Put the milk in a shallow bowl.

In a large bowl, with an electric handheld mixer, whip the cream, powdered sugar, and vanilla until stiff.

Line the bottom of the pan with a third of the whipped cream. Top with a third of the strawberries. Dip a third of the cookies quickly on both sides in the milk, then place them in a layer on top of the cookies. (Cut some of the cookies in half so the cut sides butt up against the perimeter of the pan.)

Make two more layers with the remaining whipped cream, strawberries, and cookies, ending with the cookies. Fold the overhanging baking parchment over the cake to cover, and refrigerate overnight or up to 2 days. When ready to serve, unwrap the cake and turn it out onto a serving plate. Decorate with more strawberries.

#PEANUTZONE COOKIES

With so many schools declaring themselves nut-free zones, these cookies might be contraband in some places, but they are such a miracle of food science that they're worth knowing about. Plus, they are the most gluten-free cookies that ever lived, because they bypass flour (any flour) altogether. All I know is they have the most tender, (peanut-) buttery texture of any PB cookie out there, and you pretty much can't flub them up.

MAKES 24 COOKIES

1 cup smooth peanut butter (*not natural-style unless the oil is emulsified*)

2/3 cup sugar, plus 1/4 cup for rolling

1 large egg

Preheat the oven to 350°F. Line a sheet pan with baking parchment or nonstick foil.

In a medium bowl, combine the peanut butter, 2/3 cup of the sugar, and the egg and use a silicone spatula or large spoon to blend until everything is smooth.

Pour the remaining 1/4 cup sugar onto a small plate. Using your hands, roll the dough into little balls the size of a walnut. Roll the dough balls one at a time in the sugar to coat evenly, and place them about 2 inches apart on the sheet pan. (If you're using a small sheet pan, you'll need to bake these in two batches.) Use a fork to press down on each dough ball to make a crisscross impression and to flatten them slightly.

Bake for 10 to 12 minutes, or until the cookies are set in the middle and browned around the edges. Let cool on the sheet pan for a few minutes before using a spatula to transfer them to a cooling rack or a large plate to cool completely.

TIP *If you want to make them prettier, press one chocolate kiss candy onto the top instead of marking them with a fork—or mix in some chocolate chips, or make an indentation in the center with your fingertip and put a teaspoon of grape jelly in it before baking, or sprinkle the tops with a bit of flaky salt before they go into the oven.*

TIP *Save the extra egg white to scramble on its own, or use it in the savory granola on page 106.*

HOT CHOCOLATE LAVA CAKES

BAKED IN A MUG

These chocolicious cakes are about as impressive a culinary masterpiece as you're likely to pull off in a small space. On the outside they look like any other little chocolate cakes, but as you cut into them, melting chocolate spiced with a tongue-tingling hit of cayenne (if you want it spicy) bubbles forth like a slow sweet lava flow. Very impressive indeed, but not at all tricky. Even if they're a little under- or over-baked, you still get a trophy for mastering this feat of mug-dessert engineering. Just remember not to overmix the batter.

SERVES 2

Nonstick cooking spray

½ cup *(3 ounces)* chopped semisweet chocolate

6 tablespoons *(¾ stick)* unsalted butter, in small pieces

2 tablespoons powdered sugar, plus more for dusting

1 teaspoon instant espresso powder, such as Café Bustelo

¼ teaspoon cayenne *(optional)*

1 large egg plus 1 egg yolk

2 tablespoons all-purpose flour

Ice cream, for serving *(optional)*

Preheat the oven to 400°F. Spray two 6-ounce coffee mugs with nonstick cooking spray and set them aside on a small sheet pan.

Put the chocolate in a medium heatproof bowl and microwave at 30-second intervals, stirring in between, until completely melted, about 1 to 1½ minutes total.

Add the butter, powdered sugar, espresso powder, and cayenne (if using) to the bowl with the chocolate and whisk until smooth. Add the egg and the yolk and whisk to incorporate. Add the flour and gently whisk just until combined, but do not overmix or the cakes will become rubbery (a few lumps are okay).

Use a silicone spatula to divide the batter evenly between the two mugs. (At this point, you can cover the mugs and refrigerate them for up to 12 hours to bake later.)

Bake the mug cakes on the sheet pan for exactly 10 minutes. Remove from the oven and let them cool for 5 minutes. When the mugs are cool enough to handle, run a knife around the inside of the mugs to loosen the cakes, and invert them onto small plates. Dust with additional powdered sugar and serve immediately—preferably with ice cream, if you have some around.

ACED-IT BARS

These cookie/candy bars are ridiculously easy to make. Everything happens in the baking dish by layering each ingredient on top of the next like Roman ruins. I learned how to make them at Girl Scout camp in middle school and now I bake them for my son when he aces an exam (which is not often, but the incentive is there). You could substitute any nut—or more chocolate chips—for the peanuts, and double the recipe to bake it in a 9 × 13-inch baking dish.

MAKES EIGHT 2 × 3-INCH BARS

4 tablespoons
(½ stick) salted butter

¾ cup graham cracker crumbs or cookie crumbs

¾ cup semisweet chocolate chips

½ cup ridged potato chips, crushed

⅓ cup salted peanuts, roughly chopped

½ cup shredded, sweetened coconut

¾ cup sweetened condensed milk

1 teaspoon instant espresso powder

Preheat the oven or toaster oven to 350°F.

Put the butter in an 8 × 6-inch baking dish and heat it in the oven until the butter has melted. Using oven mitts or dish towels, remove the dish from the oven and swirl it around so the butter covers the bottom evenly.

Sprinkle the graham cracker crumbs evenly over the butter, followed by even layers of the chocolate chips, potato chips, peanuts, and coconut.

In a small bowl, combine the condensed milk and espresso powder and whisk with a fork or wire whisk until smooth. Pour this mixture evenly over the top layer of coconut in the baking dish.

Bake for 25 to 30 minutes, or until the top is browned and bubbly. Let cool completely before cutting into bars directly in the baking dish. You can store the bars in an airtight container at room temperature for a week, or refrigerated for 2 weeks.

DULCE DE LECHE

Say it: DOOL se de LECH eh. The name means a sweet candy made of milk, and it's a staple all over Latin America, the way Nutella is to most of the world. It has a silky-smooth texture and a sweet, milky caramel flavor. You can pour it over ice cream or yogurt, spread it on toast or saltines or Chickpea Pancakes (page 84), stir it into coffee or Hack-uccinos (page 116), dip strawberries into it, or make the Dirty Dulce Chill Cake on page 126.

MAKES 1¼ CUPS

1 (14-ounce) can sweetened condensed milk

MAKE IT ON THE STOVE: In a small, deep saucepan with a lid, place the unopened can of condensed milk and fill the saucepan with water so that the can is totally submerged. Cover and bring the water to a boil over medium heat. Reduce the heat to low and simmer for exactly 2½ hours.

Let the can cool completely before you open it. Once opened, transfer the dulce de leche to a storage container, cover, and refrigerate for up to 1 month.

MAKE IT IN A SLOW COOKER: Place the unopened can of condensed milk in the center of the slow cooker and fill the pot with water so that the can is totally submerged. Cover and cook on Low for 6 hours.

Let the can cool completely before you open it. You can do this with as many cans as will fit in the slow cooker without crowding it.

LET'S GET READY TO CRUMMMBBBLLLLE!

When I was in elementary school, the cafeteria food was awful, with one exception: One of the cafeteria ladies made homemade apple crumble with vanilla ice cream on Fridays. It made suffering through the stinky fish sticks worthwhile. The apples were sweet but not too sweet and the crumble topping tasted like Brown Sugar Cinnamon Pop Tarts, which were a universal obsession. I found a recipe for something similar in one of my mom's cookbooks and tweaked it over and over until it tasted like the cafeteria lady's. I still make it exactly the same way. Make a batch of topping and keep it in the fridge. When you're ready to crumble, all you have to do is a quick fruit prep and pop it in the oven. A scoop of ice cream is never out of place here.

MAKES THREE 12-OUNCE MUGS OR ONE 8 × 6-INCH CRUMBLE

¼ cup granulated sugar

2 tablespoons cornstarch

4 cups whole berries, chunky unsweetened applesauce, or diced fruit such as peaches or plums

Juice of 1 lemon

STREUSEL

¾ cup all-purpose flour

¼ cup regular rolled or quick-cooking oats

⅓ cup packed light brown sugar

½ teaspoon kosher salt

½ teaspoon ground cinnamon

4 tablespoons (½ *stick*) unsalted butter, melted

Nonstick cooking spray

TO BAKE IN MUGS: Preheat the oven to 350°F.

In a small bowl, combine the granulated sugar and cornstarch and stir to blend. Add the fruit and lemon juice and toss to combine. Set aside while you make the streusel.

To make the streusel: In a large bowl, combine the flour, oats, brown sugar, salt, and cinnamon. Gradually pour in the butter and toss everything together with a fork until the mixture forms clumps but is not dry. (Get in there and work it with your fingertips until it's the right texture.) At this point, the streusel can be stored in an airtight container in the fridge for up to 1 month.

Spray 3 large coffee mugs with nonstick cooking spray.

Divide the fruit mixture among the mugs, cover with foil, and bake for 15 minutes. Uncover and stir the fruit gently to get the juices distributed. Spoon 2 to 3 tablespoons of the streusel over each mug's fruit to cover it and return the mugs to the oven. Bake for 15 to 20 minutes more, or until the fruit is bubbly and the streusel is nice and browned.

TO BAKE IN AN 8 × 6-INCH BAKING DISH:
Follow the directions above, but bake the fruit for 20 to 25 minutes before you add the streusel, and 20 to 25 minutes more after you add the streusel.

NOTE *Raising your sheet pan up on a rack or on top of scrunched up balls of foil in the skillet and closing the lid simulates the radiant heat of an oven. And what's mind blowing is that the temperature inside the skillet is exactly the same as in the oven! So if a recipe calls for baking something in a 350 °F oven, bake it in an electric skillet set at 350 °F (with a rack). The only difference is that the top won't brown.*

ESPRESSO BROWNIES

VG

Here is one really good reason to get yourself an electric skillet: You can bake in it. I've given the instructions for baking these brownies in both an oven and an electric skillet with steam (see Note), which results in brownies that have the texture of a dense flourless chocolate cake. *#BIGYUM*. Corn bread and cakes (which don't need to brown) bake really well in the skillet, too.

MAKES SIXTEEN 1½ × 2¼-INCH BROWNIES

Nonstick cooking spray

1½ sticks *(6 ounces)* unsalted butter, melted

1 cup packed brown sugar

½ cup granulated sugar

2 teaspoons vanilla extract

½ teaspoon kosher salt

3 large eggs

2 teaspoons instant espresso powder

¾ cup unsweetened cocoa powder

½ cup all-purpose flour

BAKE IT IN AN OVEN: Preheat the oven to 350°F. Spray an ⅛-size sheet pan with nonstick cooking spray.

In a large bowl, combine the butter, brown sugar, and granulated sugar and whisk vigorously for 1 minute until smooth. Add the vanilla, salt, and eggs and whisk to combine, until the eggs are mixed in. Add the espresso powder and cocoa and whisk until no visible lumps remain.

Use a large spoon or silicone spatula to gently fold in the flour just until no white streaks remain.

Spread the batter into the sheet pan in an even layer (use a silicone spatula to smooth it out if necessary) and bake for 25 to 30 minutes,

or until the edges are firm and the center is still a bit wobbly (it will firm up as it cools). Let the brownies cool completely, then cut them into whatever size or shape you're feeling. The brownies can be stored in an airtight container at room temperature for up to a week.

BAKE IT IN AN ELECTRIC SKILLET: Place a cooling rack or scrunched up foil in an electric skillet. Pour 1 cup of water into the skillet and heat it to 350°F.

Follow the directions above (but skip preheating the oven) up until you've poured the batter into the sheet pan. Place the sheet pan with the batter on top of the rack, then cover the skillet and bake for 40 minutes.

Uncover and bake for about 5 minutes more, until the edges are firm and the center is still a bit wobbly (it will firm up as it cools). Place the sheet pan on a cooling rack and let the brownies cool completely before cutting with a knife.

SHEET PAN
SHORTBREAD COOKIES

I learned the formula for real English shortbread when I was at culinary school in London, and it works perfectly every single time. You need a kitchen scale. It's 4 ounces (1 part) sugar and 8 ounces (2 parts) butter, then 4 ounces (1 part) fine semolina or rice flour and 8 ounces (2 parts) all-purpose flour. Scale it up or down but always in the same proportions. Brilliant. I've converted the recipe from weights to dry measurements so you don't have to buy a scale. It's still brilliant and a little box of homemade shortbread makes a thoughtful gift indeed.

MAKES SIXTEEN 1½ × 2-INCH BARS

2 sticks *(8 ounces)* salted butter, at room temperature

½ cup sugar, plus more for sprinkling

2 cups all-purpose flour

½ cup rice flour or fine semolina

Preheat the oven or toaster oven to 275°F.

In a large bowl, use a wooden spoon to combine the butter and ½ cup of the sugar until well blended and creamy.

Add the all-purpose flour and rice flour and stir to incorporate, until the dough is smooth and no streaks remain.

Press the dough into an ⅛-size sheet pan in an even layer and poke the dough several times (every couple of inches) with a fork. Sprinkle the top with an additional 2 tablespoons of sugar, if you like.

Bake for 1 to 1¼ hours, or until the shortbread is set and very pale brown all over. If it isn't, keep baking until it is, another 5 to 10 minutes.

Remove the shortbread from the oven and, while it's still in the pan, immediately cut into bars or squares with a sharp knife. Cool the cookies for 15 minutes in the sheet pan before transferring them to a cooling rack or platter to cool completely. The cookies can be stored at room temperature in an airtight container for up to 2 weeks, or in the freezer for up to 1 month.

Variations

GREEN TEA AND SESAME: Follow the recipe, but use the rice flour instead of semolina. Stir 1 teaspoon of powdered matcha or Chinese green tea powder into the flour before adding it to the butter mixture. Once the batter is spread out in the sheet pan, sprinkle it with white or black sesame seeds and 2 tablespoons of sugar before baking.

LEMON AND FENNEL: Follow the recipe, but add the grated zest of one lemon and 1½ teaspoons of crushed fennel seeds (put them in a zipper storage bag and bash with something heavy to break them up a bit) to the butter mixture. Use the semolina instead of rice flour. Once the batter is spread out in the sheet pan, sprinkle the batter with an additional 2 tablespoons of sugar before baking.

COFFEE AND CARDAMOM: Follow the recipe, but add 1 teaspoon of ground cardamom and 2 teaspoons of instant espresso powder to the butter mixture before adding the flour. Once the batter is spread out in the sheet pan, sprinkle the batter with 2 tablespoons of Demerara or raw sugar before baking.

SAUCES & STAPLES

CHOCOLATE GANACHE

If you're a Chocolate Person, you need to keep this stuff around. It could not be easier and it keeps in the fridge for a month. Ganache (say it: "guh-NOSH") is the chameleon of all things sweet. Here are some of the ways to use it: Keep it in your rice cooker or slow cooker on the Warm setting for fondue to dip fruit, marshmallows, and chunks of cake into; stir a couple of generous tablespoons into a mug of nearly boiling milk for hot chocolate, or blend it into a Hack-uccino (page 116); pour it, still warm, over a cake as a glaze or as hot fudge on ice cream; wait till it cools and use it as a frosting for cakes and cupcakes or sandwich it between peanut butter cookies (page 127).

MAKES 1½ CUPS

8 ounces chopped semisweet chocolate *(1 heaping cup)*

1 cup heavy cream, at room temperature

In a glass or other microwave-safe bowl, microwave the chocolate at 30-second intervals, stirring after each interval, until the chocolate is melted. Add the cream and microwave for 30 seconds more. Remove the bowl from the microwave and gently whisk the cream and chocolate until completely smooth.

Use immediately, or let the ganache cool before storing, covered, in the fridge for up to 1 month.

MAKE IT ON THE STOVE: Chop the chocolate finely. In a small saucepan, bring the cream to a boil. Immediately remove from the heat, add the chocolate (don't stir), cover, and let sit for 10 minutes.

Stir gently with a whisk until combined and no white streaks remain. (If you whisk too vigorously, it will lose its shine—but it will still be good!)

MAKE IT IN A RICE COOKER: Turn on the rice cooker to the Cook mode and pour the cream into it. Cover and wait until the cream forms tiny bubbles ever so slightly around the edges, about 4 minutes.

Remove the pan from the rice cooker and add the chocolate to the hot cream. Cover again and let the cream and chocolate sit for 5 minutes. By this time, the chocolate will have melted in the heat of the cream. Whisk gently until no lumps remain.

Use immediately, or let the ganache cool before storing, covered, in the fridge for up to 1 month.

TIP *Scoop little balls of the chilled ganache with a tiny ice cream scoop, roll in unsweetened cocoa powder, and voilà—chocolate truffles! Store them in the fridge until just before you're ready to serve them.*

BANG BANG SAUCE

GF VE DF

It's super simple to make peanut sauce that hits four of the six basic flavors: sweet, sour, salty, and umami—that difficult to describe, deeply savory one. This is the sauce used for the Bang Bang Chicken (page 50), but you can also use it on hot or cold noodles, as a dip for Rice Paper Salad Rolls (page 88), as a sauce for grilled chicken satay skewers, or as a dressing on salads. I like it on cucumbers with roughly chopped cilantro and red pepper flakes. Make a lot of it; it keeps for one month in the fridge.

MAKES 1½ CUPS

½ cup smooth peanut butter

3 tablespoons tamari or soy sauce

2 tablespoons apple cider vinegar or rice vinegar

2 tablespoons packed brown sugar

2 tablespoons toasted sesame oil

¼ cup hot water

In a medium bowl, whisk the peanut butter, tamari, vinegar, brown sugar, and sesame oil until completely smooth. Add the hot water, a little at a time, until incorporated.

Use immediately, or store the sauce in a covered jar at room temperature for up to 1 week, or refrigerated for up to 1 month. Bring to room temperature before using, or zap it in the microwave for about 15 seconds or so, until it loosens up.

PIRI PIRI SAUCE

Piri Piri Sauce is a true culinary collab; chiles from Africa, combined with paprika, vinegar, and garlic, the staples of Portuguese cooking. Here's a bit of culinary anthropology for you: Fiery malagueta peppers were discovered in the Caribbean by Portuguese explorers in the fifteenth century. The voyage of Vasco da Gama in 1498 brought the Portuguese to Africa, along with the newly discovered chiles; they then grew wild for centuries. Piri piri chiles are descended from these, and are now cultivated commercially in Zambia, Uganda, Malawi, Namibia, and Zimbabwe. Use this for the Piri Piri Chicken Lollipops (page 73), but also as a sauce for any meat, poultry, fish, or grain bowl, or simply as a dip.

MAKES 1½ CUPS

1 small red bell pepper, quartered; seeds and membranes removed

6 Fresno, cayenne, or red jalapeño chilies, halved; stems, seeds and membranes removed

4 garlic cloves

2 teaspoons kosher salt

2 tablespoons sweet smoked paprika

2 tablespoons apple cider vinegar or sherry vinegar

2 tablespoons extra-virgin olive oil

In a blender or bullet, combine the bell pepper, chilies, garlic, salt, paprika, vinegar, and olive oil and blend until smooth, stopping to scrape down the sides with a silicone spatula, about 30 seconds total.

Transfer the sauce to a glass jar and keep covered and refrigerated for up to 1 month.

CORE TOMATO SAUCE

I mean, you won't take a bath in this Greatest of All Time sauce, but you'll use it for everything else. Almost. My grandmother never *didn't* have some of this around. It's a simple, comforting sauce to ladle over pasta or simmer chicken pieces or cannellini beans in, with some spinach added at the end. With this on hand, Shakshuka (page 23), One-Pot Pasta with Sausage & Broccoli (page 45), and "Cheaters Never Prosper" Baked Ravioli Lasagne (page 40) are a quick fix. An electric skillet or slow cooker is ideal for this; the sauce pretty much takes care of itself, except for the occasional stir and encouraging word from you.

MAKES ABOUT 3 CUPS

1 (28-ounce) can whole peeled tomatoes, squished up *(use your hands)*

2 garlic cloves, halved

1 medium onion, roughly chopped

¼ cup extra-virgin olive oil or 4 tablespoons (½ stick) unsalted butter *(DON'T skimp; this is what makes it so good)*

1 teaspoon kosher salt

You can either leave the sauce chunky, or let cool and blend with an immersion blender or transfer to a blender or food processor to blend to your desired texture.

The sauce will keep covered in the fridge for 1 week, or frozen for up to 2 months.

MAKE IT ON THE STOVE: In a large saucepan over medium heat, combine the tomatoes, garlic, onion, olive oil, and salt. Cover the saucepan and cook, stirring occasionally, until the onion and garlic are very soft and the sauce is thickened, about 1 hour. The fat will rise to the surface but just stir the sauce to blend everything again. Taste and season with additional salt, as desired.

MAKE IT IN AN ELECTRIC SKILLET: Combine all of the ingredients in an electric skillet preheated to 300°F. Follow the directions above.

MAKE IT IN A SLOW COOKER: Combine all of the ingredients in the slow cooker and set it to Low. Follow the directions above, but cook the sauce for 6 hours.

SWEET TOMATO CHUTNEY

Go get a spoon, any spoon, and I'll teach you the easiest way to peel ginger. Hold the spoon perpendicular to the ginger and scrape the ginger with the edge of the spoon. The outside layer will peel right off, even from the little nubbins. Now you're ready to make this sweet, spicy, and tangy chutney. It's good with soft cheese, as a spread on sandwiches (especially grilled cheese), as a condiment on rice and beans, or wrapped up with a ribbon as a gift. *#skillz*

MAKES 2½ CUPS

1 (*15-ounce*) can diced tomatoes

1 tablespoon peeled and grated ginger

1 small onion, chopped

2 garlic cloves, chopped

2 teaspoons garam masala

4 tablespoons apple cider vinegar or rice vinegar

¾ cup sugar

1 teaspoon kosher salt

¼ teaspoon cayenne, or more to taste

Combine the tomatoes, ginger, onion, garlic, garam masala, vinegar, sugar, salt, and cayenne in a medium saucepan and stir over medium heat until the sugar is dissolved, about 3 minutes. Taste and add more cayenne if you like it spicier.

Turn the heat up to maintain a gentle boil and cook for about 45 minutes, stirring every once in a while, until the chutney has thickened and is the consistency of jam.

Serve warm, or keep covered in the fridge for up to 2 months.

MAKE IT IN A RICE COOKER: Make sure your rice cooker has a capacity of at least 4 cups. Cook the chutney for one cycle on the Cook mode, stir, and cook it for another cycle, about 50 minutes total.

MAKE IT IN A SLOW COOKER: Double or triple the recipe and cook it in a slow cooker on Low for 6 hours.

PICKLED TINK ONIONS

GF VE DF

You'll be tickled pink by how easy and delicious these are. They're a puckery addition to everything from Falafel Burgers (page 98), Keema (page 74), Black Beans & Rice (page 47), and Bollywood Butter Chicken (page 76) to soups, salads, and my favorite: hot dogs.

MAKES ABOUT 2 CUPS

1 large red onion, thinly sliced

2 teaspoons kosher salt

2/3 cup distilled white vinegar

Dash of cayenne *(optional)*

In a medium bowl or a lidded jar, combine the onions and salt and toss gently to combine. Let the onions sit for about 30 minutes, until they start to "weep" (release their juices).

Add the vinegar and the cayenne (if using), cover, and let the onions continue to sit at room temperature for at least 2 hours. The longer they sit, the pinker they will become—it's up to you!

The pickled onions can be kept covered in the fridge for up to 1 month.

TEAKETTLE EGG

A bit of trivia: 2 quarts of water take 10 minutes to come to a boil in a saucepan, or 3 minutes in an electric teakettle (and it turns itself off!). You can boil up to 6 eggs at a time this way, and then drink the water or use it to make tea or coffee. Eggshells have long been used as a water purifier, and the calcium and minerals that leach into the water from the eggshells help support healthy bones. *#WinWin*

SERVES 1

1 large egg

Fill an electric kettle a quarter of the way full with water and carefully lower an egg into it. Fill the kettle with additional water until the egg is covered by at least 1 inch.

Close the kettle and turn it on. After the kettle boils and rings, let the egg sit in the hot water for 3 to 4 minutes for a soft-boiled egg, 5 to 6 minutes for a jammy egg, and 7 to 9 minutes for hard-boiled.

Use a long spoon or tongs to remove the egg from the water, and run it under cold water.

TIP *Eggs become easier to peel the older they get. To tell how fresh an egg is, put it in a glass of water: super fresh and it sinks to the bottom; less fresh but good to eat and it stands up on end but still touches the bottom; if it floats, it's compost.*

ACKNOWLEDGMENTS

Thanks first of all to Dimity Jones, who brought this project to me; to Hannah Rahill, who greenlighted it; and to Lydia O'Brien, who made the editing process 99 percent less traumatic than I feared. Thank you to Martha Hopkins for her superior agenting skills, to Devon Donohue and my nieces Sydney Walley, Jenny Black, and Samantha Walley for their educated palates and recipe testing, and to my assistant, Sofie Taddeo, who shopped, tested, cooked, styled, and hand-modeled her way through this project with grace and good cheer. Thank you to Marysarah Quinn and Jen Wang for their keen eye and good taste, to Emily Schindler for bringing this project to life through her lens, and to Julie Bernouis for her prop styling and buoyant spirit. Thank you to Kerri Brewer and Paige Hicks (sorry about the Vitamix blade; it will be replaced) and to my surly but lovable son, Theo, who wishes I would for once just cook something normal.

INDEX